Fabulous Fun Facts for Inquisitive Kids:

1,000+ Truths About History, Science, Culture and Nature with Quizzes and Would You Rather Questions

Violet L Wilson

© Copyright 2024 - All rights reserved.

The content contained within this book may not be reproduced, duplicated or transmitted without direct written permission from the author or the publisher. Under no circumstances will any blame or legal responsibility be held against the publisher, or author, for any damages, reparation, or monetary loss due to the information contained within this book, either directly or indirectly.

Legal Notice:

This book is copyright protected. It is only for personal use. You cannot amend, distribute, sell, use, quote or paraphrase any part, or the content within this book, without the consent of the author or publisher.

Disclaimer Notice:

Please note the information contained within this document is for educational and entertainment purposes only. All effort has been executed to present accurate, up to date, reliable, complete information. No warranties of any kind are declared or implied. Readers acknowledge that the author is not engaged in the rendering of legal, financial, medical or professional advice. The content within this book has been derived from various sources. Please consult a licensed professional before attempting any techniques outlined in this book.

By reading this document, the reader agrees that under no circumstances is the author responsible for any losses, direct or indirect, that are incurred as a result of the use of the information contained within this document, including, but not limited to, errors, omissions, or inaccuracies.

Contents

Introduction 7

Chapter One

The Wacky World of Animals 8

Chapter Two

Fantastic Feats of the Human Body 30

Chapter Three

Marvelous Marvels of Nature 48

Chapter Four

Astounding Astronomy and Sensational Space 66

Chapter Five

Phenomenal Physical Forces 82

Chapter Six

Inventions That Changed Our World 98

Chapter Seven

Delightful Discoveries in Math and Numbers 114

Chapter Eight

Scrumptious Science of Food 122

Chapter Nine

Mysteries of History 138

Chapter Ten

Odds and Ends... 158

Conclusion..174

What Next? 177

Quiz Answers..179

References 190

Introduction

Hey there! Welcome to a world full of amazing facts and fun questions that will blow your mind. Whether you're curious about space, animals, history, or just love a good challenge, there's something here for you. And guess what? It's not just about reading; it's about having a blast while doing it!

So why are fun facts so awesome? First, they're like little nuggets of wisdom that make you go, "Wow, I didn't know that!" Did you know that honey never spoils? A jar of honey could sit on your shelf for thousands of years and still be delicious! Or that an octopus has three hearts? Mind-blowing, right? Facts like these are super cool to share and make you look like a genius.

Not only do these facts make you smarter, but they also give you something incredible to talk about. Imagine being at a family dinner or a school lunch and dropping a fun fact like, "Did you know that bananas are berries, but strawberries aren't?" Everyone's going to stop and say, "Wait, what? Tell me more!" You'll have all eyes on you, and that's pretty awesome.

Every chapter ends with a quiz – yes answers are in the back of the book – and would you rather questions, These questions are like mini adventures that get everyone involved. For example, would you rather have the ability to fly or be invisible? Questions like this spark debates and bring out everyone's imagination. They're perfect for road trips, sleepovers, or just hanging out at home.

So dive in and explore! Whether you're stumping your friends with tricky riddles or impressing your family with wild facts, this book is your ticket to endless fun and discovery. Get ready to amaze, entertain, and become the go-to person for fascinating knowledge. Let's kick off this adventure and see where it takes you!

Chapter One

The Wacky World of Animals

The Animal Kingdom: A Diverse World

Understanding the incredible world of mammals is like opening a door to endless wonders. These creatures, seen daily in our lives, possess unique traits and abilities that set them apart in the animal kingdom. From the nimble bats navigating the night sky with their extraordinary echolocation to the grand elephants with their unmatched memory and intricate social networks, each mammal has adapted to its environment in fascinating ways.

In this chapter, we'll delve into some truly extraordinary examples of mammalian diversity. By exploring these amazing stories, you'll gain a deeper appreciation for the incredible adaptability and specialized skills that make every mammal unique in its way.

Extraordinary Mammals

When you think of mammals, you might picture a dog or a cat, but the world of mammals is incredibly diverse. Each species has evolved specialized skills that enable them to thrive in their environments. Whether it's the echolocation of bats, the social complexity of elephants, or the advanced communication of dolphins, these mammals demonstrate the sheer diversity of the animal kingdom.

Here are some extraordinary facts about mammals:

- Mammals are warm-blooded vertebrates (animals that can keep a high and constant body temperature).
- The tallest mammal is a giraffe at 20 feet. Not only are they tall, but they have long tongues which they use to pick their nose—yuck!
- The fastest mammal on land is a cheetah, which can run at top speeds of up to 75 miles per hour and can get from 0 to 60 miles per hour in under 3 seconds! The fastest human is left well behind with a top speed of about 27 miles per hour.
- There are approximately 6,400 different species of mammal, which belong to the class Mammalia.
- The fastest mammal in water is the dolphin, which swims at speeds up to 37 miles per hour.
- Polar bears look white but their skin is actually black.
- Most mammals give live birth, except for monotremes (a primitive form of mammal that lays eggs) like the platypus and echidna.
- Mammals are remarkably adaptive animals because of the different evolutionary requirements they've had to meet over the past 50 million years: Some swim, others fly, and some even burrow or climb!
- They possess specialized teeth adapted to their diet (e.g., carnivores have sharper teeth, herbivores have flatter teeth).
- Bats are the only mammals capable of sustained flight and can fly at speeds of 60 miles per hour.

→ Mammals generally seek companionship, often living in groups or packs.

Here's a list of mammals that are known by unexpected or surprising terms:

Animal	Group
Hippos	A bloat of hippos
Giraffes	A tower of giraffes
Apes	A shrewdness of apes
Bats	A cauldron of bats
Pandas	An embarrassment of pandas

→ Mammals are the best parents in the animal kingdom, as their young are born helpless and need a lot of care in the first few months of their lives.

→ Mammals have a highly developed brain relative to their body size.

→ Echolocation (a process where animals sense their surroundings through uttering and listening to sound waves) is used by some mammals, including bats and dolphins, to navigate and hunt.

→ Mammals evolved from "mammal-like reptiles" called therapsids that lived around 230 million years ago during the late Triassic period.

→ The smallest known mammal is the bumblebee bat, weighing about 0.07 ounces.

→ The blue whale (*Balaenoptera musculus*) is the largest mammal living today. It can grow up to 110 feet long and weigh more than 330,000 pounds!

→ Mammals are an important part of the ecosystem. Through their activities, plants are pollinated, seeds are dispersed, and pests are under control!

→ Some mammals, like the polar bear, have adapted to extremely cold environments with specialized insulating fur.

Surprising Facts

Did you know that male seahorses are the ones that get pregnant and carry the babies? They have a special pouch where females deposit their eggs and the males fertilize and incubate them until they're ready to be born. It's a unique role reversal in the animal kingdom!

One unusual fact about mammals is that the echidna and the platypus are the only egg-laying mammals, known as monotremes. While most mammals give birth to live young, these two species lay eggs and have unique characteristics, like the echidna's spiny coat and the platypus's duck-like bill.

Incredible Insects

The world of insects is filled with incredible features and survival strategies that make these tiny creatures fascinating. Insects are everywhere around us, from the garden in your backyard to deep inside the forests and even in the water. They have adapted to survive in almost every environment on Earth.

Here are some incredible facts about insects:

- Insects make up about 80% of all known animal species on Earth.
- There are approximately 1 million described species of insects, with estimates suggesting there may be over 30 million undiscovered species.
- About 400,000 out of Earth's 1 million named insect species are beetles.
- Insects have a hard exoskeleton made of chitin, which provides protection and structure.
- They breathe through tiny openings called spiracles located along the sides of their bodies.
- Some insects, like ants and bees, are social and live in complex colonies, while others prefer to be alone, like spiders or scorpions.
- Insects undergo metamorphosis (a transformation), which can be complete (egg, larva, pupa, adult) or incomplete (egg, nymph, adult). One well-known example is the transformation of a caterpillar into a beautiful butterfly!

Here's a list of unusual names for groups of insects:

Insect	Group
Butterflies	A kaleidoscope of butterflies
Grasshoppers	A cloud of grasshoppers
Spiders	A cluster of spiders
Anteaters	A candle of anteaters
Crickets	An orchestra of crickets

→ Butterflies taste with their feet, allowing them to identify suitable plants for laying eggs.

→ The dragonfly is one of the fastest insects, capable of flying at speeds up to 35 miles per hour.

→ Cockroaches can live for several weeks without their heads due to their decentralized nervous system.

→ Termites are known for their ability to digest cellulose, which allows them to break down wood.

→ The average lifespan of a housefly is about 28 days, though some can live up to 2 months.

→ Some insects have developed bioluminescence, like fireflies, which use light to attract mates.

- Insects are crucial for pollination, a process many plants need to grow. For instance, a single bee can pollinate up to 5,000 plants a day!
- Cicadas can produce sounds that reach up to 120 decibels, making it one of the loudest insects.
- Many insects have camouflage abilities to avoid predators, blending in with their surroundings. For example, the leaf katydid conceals itself by looking just like a leaf!
- Ants can lift objects up to 50 times their body weight thanks to their strong muscles and small size.
- The world's largest insect is the giant weta, which can weigh as much as a small bird.
- Some species of butterflies and moths migrate long distances; the monarch butterfly migrates up to 3,000 miles.
- Insects play a vital role in disposing of organic matter and adding nutrients back into the ecosystem. For instance, dung beetles kindly feed on our poop!
- The water strider can walk on water due to surface tension created by its long, slender legs.

Surprising Facts

Did you know that the tiny mosquito is the deadliest animal on Earth? It has been estimated that it causes around one million deaths per year!

Dragonflies are aerial acrobats that can fly in all directions, including flying backward and hovering.

Amazing Amphibians and Reptiles

Amphibians and reptiles are some of the world's most amazing creatures as they are extremely adaptable. Amphibians can live both in water and on land, while reptiles have adapted to diverse environments, from deserts to rainforests. They play vital roles in ecosystems, such as controlling insect populations, serving as prey for other animals, and contributing to nutrient cycling in their environments. In particular, amphibians are often considered indicators of environmental health because they are sensitive to changes in their habitat, which highlights the need for conservation efforts.

The facts below demonstrate the complexity and importance of amphibians and reptiles to the world's ecosystem:

- → Both amphibians and reptiles are ectothermic (cold-blooded), meaning they rely on external heat sources to regulate their body temperatures.
- → Amphibians have permeable skin that allows them to absorb water and breathe through it, while reptiles have dry, scaly skin that helps retain moisture.
- → Many amphibians, like frogs, undergo a life cycle that includes a metamorphosis from a larval stage, such as a tadpole, to an adult form.
- → There are more than 8,000 species of amphibians and nearly 10,000 species of reptiles worldwide.
- → The word "amphibian" comes from the Greek term *amphibious*, meaning to "live a double life."

- Some amphibians exhibit complex parental behaviors, such as carrying their young on their backs or guarding their eggs. For instance, the strawberry poison-dart frog dad guards eggs and pees on them every day to keep them moist.
- Brightly colored patterns in amphibians can serve as a warning to the most venomous or poisonous predators about their toxicity, while many reptiles use camouflage for protection.
- Some amphibians can live for several decades in the wild; for example, certain species of frogs and salamanders can live over 30 years. For instance, the African clawed frog can live for 20–30 years in captivity.
- While most reptiles are not venomous, some, like snakes, have developed venomous mechanisms for hunting and self-defense. The most venomous snake is the Australian inland taipan. One of its bites can kill multiple mice!
- Reptiles lay eggs with protective shells (amniotic eggs) that allow them to reproduce in terrestrial environments, unlike most amphibians that need water for laying eggs.
- Reptiles are part of an ancient lineage that dates back over 300 million years, making them one of the oldest groups of vertebrates.
- Some amphibians—such as Cope's gray tree frogs—can survive freezing temperatures by entering a state of dormancy and producing antifreeze proteins in their bodies.
- Amphibians mainly eat insects and animals, while reptiles have varied diets, with some eating only plants and others only eating insects and animals.

- Most reptiles have movable eyelids, while many amphibians, like frogs, have a transparent membrane protecting their eyes instead.
- Amphibians often communicate using vocalizations. Frogs are known for their croaking, while some reptiles use body language or head bobbing to signal aggression or submission.
- Amphibians are more sensitive to environmental changes and are often found in more humid, temperate regions, whereas reptiles can thrive in a variety of climates.
- Many amphibians and reptiles, such as the boreal chorus frog, undergo hibernation or brumation during extreme weather, slowing their metabolic rates to conserve energy.
- Some species of amphibians, like the axolotl, can regenerate lost limbs, and certain reptiles can regrow their tails after losing them.
- The most venomous amphibians have specialized skin glands that secrete toxins to deter predators and protect themselves in the wild. The tiny golden dart frog contains enough poison to kill 20,000 mice!
- Amphibians are among the most endangered groups of animals due to habitat loss, pollution, climate change, and disease.

Here are some unusual terms for groups of amphibians and reptiles:

Amphibian or Reptile	Group
Newts	An armada of newts
Salamanders	A herd or congress of salamanders
Frogs	An army or a colony of frogs
Snakes or vipers	A nest of snakes or vipers
Crocodiles	A bask of crocodiles

Surprising Facts

Geckos can detach its tail to wriggle and move on their own to distract predators and give them a chance to escape.

Many reptiles, such as turtles and crocodiles, can breathe through their butts, a process known as cloacal respiration, which allows them to extract oxygen from water while remaining underwater.

Underwater Wonders

The underwater world is a vast and mysterious realm, teeming with life and diversity. It includes oceans, seas, lakes, and rivers, each hosting unique ecosystems. Coral reefs, often referred to as the "rainforests of the sea," are among the most vibrant environments, supporting a myriad of species. Deep-sea creatures, like bioluminescent fish and giant squids, thrive in complete darkness and extreme pressure, showcasing nature's adaptability.

Marine life is an incredible testament to the adaptability and diversity of nature. The underwater world is full of fascinating creatures, each with unique qualities designed to help them survive in their environment. It ranges from tiny plankton to the gigantic blue whale. Other wonders are colorful fish, graceful sea turtles, and playful dolphins. The underwater landscape features stunning formations such as kelp forests, underwater volcanoes, and shipwrecks. Human impact, such as pollution and overfishing, poses a threat to these ecosystems, making conservation efforts crucial to preserving the beauty and balance of the underwater world.

Let's look at some interesting facts about marine life:

- The ocean covers about 71% of the Earth's surface.
- More than 230,000 marine species have been identified, with many more yet to be discovered.
- The blue whale is the largest animal on the planet, reaching lengths of up to 100 feet.
- Coral reefs are home to about 25% of all marine species.
- Sea turtles have existed for over 100 million years and can hold their breath for several hours.

- Octopuses have three hearts and blue blood because their blood contains copper instead of iron, unlike human blood.
- The deepest part of the ocean, the Mariana Trench, is about 36,000 feet deep.
- Some species of fish, like the clownfish, can change their gender during their lifetime.
- Jellyfish have been around for more than 500 million years, making them older than dinosaurs.
- The box jellyfish is the most venomous creature in the world.
- At 216,672 miles, the Great Barrier Reef in Australia is the largest coral reef system in the world.
- Bioluminescence is common in the ocean, with creatures like jellyfish producing their own light.
- Bioluminescence is used to attract prey and mates and to deter predators.
- Dolphins are known for their intelligence and can recognize themselves in mirrors.
- The octopus is capable of tasting through its suckers, and some species are masters of camouflage.
- Sea otters hold hands while sleeping to prevent drifting apart.
- Some fish, like the clownfish, have a close relationship with sea anemones for protection.
- The ocean produces over half of the world's oxygen, primarily through phytoplankton.
- Narwhals are often called "unicorns of the sea" due to their long, spiral tusks.

→ The lion's mane jellyfish has tentacles that can grow up to 120 feet long.

→ About 90% of the ocean is unexplored and unmapped.

Here is a list of unusual names for groups of marine creatures:

Marine creature	Group name
Jellyfish	A smack of jellyfish
Octopus	A consortium of octopus
Sea otters	A raft of sea otters
Fish	A school or shoal of fish
Barracuda	A battery of barracuda

Surprising Facts

Given that so much of the Earth is actually underwater, you might not be surprised to discover that an astonishing 94% of the Earth's living species live in its oceans.

Some underwater volcanoes can create "brinicles," which are underwater icicles formed when supercooled salty water descends from sea ice and freezes the surrounding seawater, creating a spectacular effect that can sometimes trap marine life beneath them.

Bizarre Birds

Birds are truly fascinating creatures! They come in a dazzling array of colors, shapes, and sizes. Their ability to fly gives them a unique perspective of the world, and their songs create beautiful symphonies in nature. Many species exhibit remarkable intelligence, problem-solving skills, and social behaviors. Plus, the variety of nests they build and their migratory patterns are simply mind-blowing. Whether it's the majestic eagle soaring through the sky or the tiny hummingbird flitting from flower to flower, birds bring joy and wonder to our lives!

Here are some fascinating facts about birds:

- Birds are warm-blooded vertebrates.
- Birds are the only animals with feathers
- Birds lay eggs that are hard-shelled.
- There are over 10,000 species of birds worldwide.
- The smallest and lightest bird is the bee hummingbird, which is native to Cuba. Adult males weigh about 0.06–0.07 ounces, making them the world's smallest and lightest bird species.
- The largest bird is the ostrich, typically standing about 8–9 feet tall and weighing between 220 and 350 pounds.
- Birds have hollow bones that make them lightweight for flying.
- Some birds are flightless. This type of bird often evolved in environments where flying was not necessary for survival, such as isolated islands or areas with few predators. This led to adaptations like stronger legs for running and

- foraging on the ground. Examples include the kiwi, emu, and the cassowary!
- Eagles have brilliant eyesight and can spot a potential dinner 2 miles away.
- Many birds can migrate thousands of miles seasonally. For example, the Arctic tern migrates the longest distance of any animal, flying 55,923 miles each year from Greenland to the Weddell Sea on the Antarctic Peninsula.
- Some birds, like the parrot, can mimic human speech. The Amazon parrot can develop a vocabulary of around 300 words and phrases.
- Penguins are flightless birds that are excellent swimmers. They can jump up to 6–7 feet out of the water and onto land. They can dive up to 1,800 feet below sea level.
- The average lifespan of a bird varies greatly, from a few years to over 50. The world's oldest bird is a 73-year-old albatross named Wisdom!
- Birds are found on every continent, including Antarctica.
- Some birds, like the albatross, can cross the world without flapping their wings, flying up to 500–600 miles in a day!
- The lyrebird is a master mimic and can imitate a variety of sounds, including chainsaws, camera shutters, and other bird calls.
- Flamingos get their pink color from the food they eat, primarily shrimp.
- The wandering albatross has the largest wingspan of any living bird, reaching up to 12 feet.
- The common raven is one of the most intelligent bird species.

→ In certain bird species, males may also participate in incubating eggs or feeding chicks.

Here's a list of unusual names for groups of birds:

Bird	Group
Raven	An unkindness or conspiracy of ravens
Finches	A trembling of finches
Buntings	A mural of buntings
Crows	A murder of crows
Wrens	A chime of wrens

Surprising Facts

Did you know that birds are descended from reptiles? It's true! The earliest known bird was the Archaeopteryx, which lived approximately 150 million years ago. It was very different from modern birds because it had a long bony tail and teeth—scary!

Penguins poop about every 20 minutes. In fact, they poop a lot, 145 times a day.

Cats and Dogs

Want to know more about our furry companions and man's best friend? Look no further! Let's explore some fun facts about cats and dogs below.

Cats

- One courageous kitty, Felicette, went to space in 1963—astronaut cat!
- Your cute kitty is basically a mini tiger. They share 95% of their DNA!
- Cats are most active at dawn and dusk. That's called being crepuscular, a fancy word for being sneaky!
- When your cat rubs their head on you, they're not just being cute; they're claiming you as their territory!
- Cats are chatterboxes. They can make around 100 different sounds, while dogs can only do about 10. That's a lot of meows!
- Wild cats bury their poop to hide their scent from predators, so when your cat does it at home, they're being super sneaky.
- Cats climb trees, but when it's time to come down, they go backward because their claws are like tree-climbing hooks.
- A cat's whiskers, which help them sense objects and communicate their mood, are like measuring tape. They spend eight hours a day cleaning themselves, and another eight hours sleeping!
- Unlike us, cats can only move their jaw up and down, no sideways chomping.

- Cats are night vision ninjas. They can see six to eight times better than you in the dark.
- Both cats and dogs have a secret weapon: a third eyelid that helps protect their eyes.

Dogs

- Dogs are like the great-great-great-grandkids of wolves. They were the first animals humans tamed, about 30,000 years ago.
- Got a good nose? Well, a dog's sense of smell is 10,000 times better than yours! They have super-smelling powers!
- Dogs smell differently through each nostril, like a "nosey superpower," and no two dogs' noses are alike, just like human fingerprints!
- Dogs can see the world in blue and yellow but miss out on red and green. It's like they live in their own colorful universe.
- Ever heard of a dog yodeling? Basenjis don't bark; they yodel! That's one fancy dog sound.
- Dogs are word geniuses, as they can learn up to 1,000 words. But they pay close attention to your tone, so talk nicely!
- Dogs sniff each other's butts to say, "hi"—kind of like their version of a handshake. It's weird but true!
- The fastest dog is the greyhound, which can sprint up to 35 miles per hour for over five miles—super speedy!
- Ever notice a dog kicking back after pooping? They're marking their territory with scent glands in their paws. It's like leaving a signature!

Chapter Two

Fantastic Feats of the Human Body

Our bodies are capable of some truly mind-blowing feats. Have you ever wondered how your heart races when you're excited or why your brain can remember that fun day at the park? This chapter is all about exploring these remarkable abilities and more.

We'll dive into the incredible power of the human heart, showcasing how it tirelessly pumps blood and supports every cell in your body. You'll also discover the amazing functions of the brain, from controlling simple tasks like breathing to handling complex ones such as decision-making. Plus, we'll explore the fantastic mechanisms behind our vision. Get ready to be amazed by the extraordinary systems and organs that keep us alive and thriving!

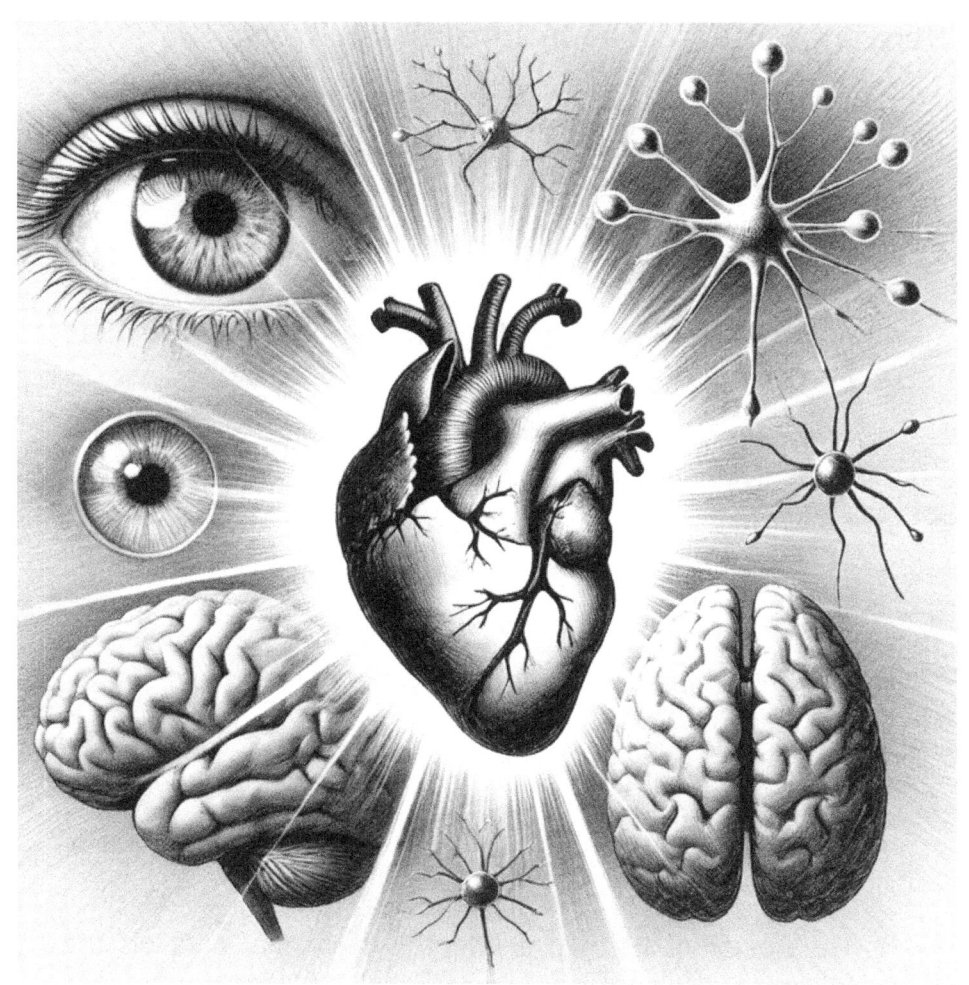

The Powerhouse Heart

The human heart is nothing short of a marvel, often referred to as the powerhouse of the body. It pumps a monumental 8,000 liters of blood each day, ensuring every cell receives the oxygen and nutrients it needs to thrive. Imagine a hardworking pump that never takes a break—that's your heart!

Here are some facts about the human heart:

- → The human heart is a muscular organ about the size of a fist. On average, the human heart weighs between 7 and 15 ounces.
- → The heart is located slightly left of center in the chest. It doesn't look heart-shaped and has been described as more like an upside-down pear.
- → The heart has four chambers: two atria and two ventricles. It is divided into left and right sides, serving different functions.
- → The right atrium receives deoxygenated blood from the body.
- → The right ventricle pumps deoxygenated blood to the lungs for oxygenation.
- → The left atrium receives oxygenated blood from the lungs.
- → The left ventricle pumps oxygenated blood to the rest of the body.
- → The heart has its own electrical system that controls the heartbeat. Hearts beat approximately 100,000 times a day.
- → The average adult heartbeat is 60– 100 beats per minute at rest.
- → The average heartbeat of a child aged 3–4 years is 70–100 beats per minute at rest.
- → The average heartbeat of a child aged 5–7 is 65–100 beats per minute.
- → Newborn babies have the fastest heartbeats with a heart rate of 70–190 beats per minute.

- The heart can pump out about 1.5 gallons of blood every minute.
- Over a lifetime, the heart can beat more than 2.5 billion times.
- There are 60,000 miles of blood vessels in the human body.
- The heart valves prevent the backflow of blood and ensure it flows in one direction. If you listen carefully you can hear them open and close.

Mind-Blowing Fact?

Surprising Facts

Did you know that the heart can continue to beat even when it's disconnected from the body? Yes, it's true. It even has its own intrinsic electrical system that controls the heartbeat.

The heart works twice as hard as a sprinter's leg muscles! Because it takes so much force to move your blood around the human body, the heart needs to be very strong to make sure all your bodily needs are met.

The Incredible Brain

Imagine your body as an incredibly well-coordinated orchestra. The brain is the conductor, guiding and controlling every instrument to create a beautiful harmony. This part of our journey dives into the marvelous world of the brain, revealing how it controls both simple and complex tasks that keep us alive and thinking.

Here are some incredible facts about the human brain:

- The human brain weighs about 3 pounds.
- It contains approximately 86 billion neurons.
- Neurons communicate through synapses, and there are about 100 trillion synapses in the brain.
- The brain consumes about 20% of the body's total energy, despite making up only about 2% of its weight.
- The left hemisphere is typically responsible for language and analytical tasks, while the right hemisphere is involved in creativity and intuition.
- The human brain is around 75% water.
- The brain can produce about 23 watts of power when awake, enough to power a small light bulb.
- The brain continues to develop until a person is around 25 years old.
- The cerebral cortex, which is responsible for higher-level functions, has a surface area similar to that of a large pizza (approximately 2.5 square feet).
- The brain can rewire itself through a process called neuroplasticity.

- Your brain is more active when you're asleep than when you're awake.
- The average adult brain has about 100 billion glial cells, which support and protect neurons.
- The human brain generates approximately 50,000 thoughts per day.
- Memory and intelligence are primarily associated with the brain's structure and networking of neurons.
- The average human intelligence quotient (IQ) is 100, with most people having an IQ between 85 and 115.
- The brain can recognize faces based on just a few features, which is part of why visual recognition is so powerful.

Surprising Facts

Did you know that your body temperature is controlled by the brain? It's true! The body temperature of all mammals is controlled by a part of the brain called the "hypothalamus." In humans, core temperature is ideally 98.6 °F (37 °C) but can range from 97 °F (36.1 °C) to 99 °F (37.2 °C).

One fascinating fact about the brain is that it has an unlimited storage capacity! That means you can't ever run out of places in your head to store new facts and information—like everything you learn in this book!

The Amazing Eyes

The human eye is an incredible organ, capable of processing the world around us in vibrant detail. It is a complex organ that allows us to perceive light and color. It consists of various parts, including the cornea, lens, retina, and iris, each playing a critical role in vision. The eye receives light and focuses it onto the retina, where photoreceptor cells convert it into neural signals sent to the brain, enabling sight.

Here are some amazing facts about the eyes:

- → The average human eye measures about 0.945 inches in diameter.
- → The cornea is the eye's outermost layer and helps to focus light.
- → The retina contains approximately 120 million rods and 6 million cones, which are responsible for vision.
- → Rods are more sensitive to light, while cones detect color and detail.
- → The human eye can distinguish about 10 million different colors.
- → The pupil can change size to control the amount of light entering the eye.
- → The eye has a blind spot where the optic nerve connects to the retina, with no photoreceptors.
- → Human eyes are capable of perceiving motion in low light conditions better than in bright light.
- → The lens changes shape to help focus on objects at various distances, a process known as accommodation.

→ Tears are produced by tear glands and help to lubricate and protect the eye.

→ The sclera, or the white part of the eye, provides structure and protection.

→ A human eye can focus on about 50 different objects per second.

→ The eye is made up of three main layers: the outer layer (sclera and cornea), the middle layer (choroid, ciliary body, and iris), and the inner layer (retina).

→ Each eye has about 6,000–7,000 sensory receptors for touch, which contribute to the perception of the eye's surface.

→ Brown is the world's most common eye color. About 79% of the world's population has brown eyes, 8–10% blue eyes, 5% hazel eyes, and 2% green eyes.

→ Eye color is determined by the amount and type of pigments in the iris, primarily melanin.

Surprising Facts

Human eyes can distinguish about 10 million different colors, but our brains can only remember about 1,000 colors clearly.

The eyelash growth cycle is fascinating; each eyelash lasts for about 3–5 months before shedding, which is why you don't lose them all at once.

Super Senses

The five senses are sight, hearing, taste, touch, and smell. They allow us to perceive and interact with the world around us. They allow us to perceive our environment, communicate with others, and experience life fully. Through these senses, we can navigate our surroundings, recognize dangers, enjoy food and relationships, and appreciate the beauty of life. They also play a vital role in our emotional responses and memory, helping us learn and adapt to various situations. Overall, our senses enrich our experiences and understanding of the world.

Here are some superb facts about our super senses:

- Humans have five main senses: sight, hearing, taste, touch, and smell.
- The sense of sight is the most dominant, making up about 80% of our sensory perception.
- Eyes see things upside down—it's the brain that turns the image right side up again.
- Your sense of taste is primarily located on your tongue but also involves your sense of smell. In the animal kingdom, elephants have the best sense of smell while dolphins have the worst.
- Taste buds can detect five basic tastes: sweet, salty, sour, bitter, and umami (savory).
- The sense of smell is closely linked to memory; certain scents can evoke strong memories and emotions.
- Humans possess a "sixth sense" that refers to the ability to perceive beyond the normal five senses, often associated with intuition.

- Touch is the first sense to develop in humans, beginning in the womb.
- There are different types of receptors in the skin that respond to various stimuli, such as pressure, temperature, and pain.
- The average human has about 2,000–8,000 taste buds, which gradually decline with age.
- Hearing is the second most important sense for communication, following vision.
- Sound travels faster in water than in air, which is why underwater sounds can seem louder.
- The human ear has three parts: the outer ear, the middle ear, and the inner ear, each playing a vital role in hearing.
- The sense of balance is located in the inner ear, specifically in the vestibular system (a sensory system in the middle ear).
- Humans can detect sounds ranging from 20 to 20,000 hertz, although this range decreases with age.
- The brain processes information from the senses in the sensory cortex, which is organized by type of sense.
- Sensory adaptation happens when our sensitivity to a sense we experience all the time decreases over time. For instance, you might get used to a strong smell.

Surprising Facts

Humans can detect a trillion different scents, thanks to a range of olfactory receptors in the nose that work together to identify various smells, which is far more than the previously thought 10,000 scents.

One surprising fact about the senses is that taste is heavily influenced by smell. In fact, up to 80% of what we perceive as taste actually comes from our sense of smell. This is why food can taste bland when you have a blocked nose!

Eating and Digestion

Eating and digestion are essential processes that allow our bodies to obtain and utilize nutrients from the food we consume. When we eat, food is broken down into smaller pieces by chewing, mixed with saliva, and then swallowed. It travels down the esophagus to the stomach, where it is combined with gastric acids and enzymes to further break it down into a semi-liquid form called chyme. The chyme then moves into the small intestine, where the majority of digestion and nutrient absorption occurs. The pancreas and liver contribute digestive enzymes and bile to help with this process. Nutrients are absorbed through the intestinal walls into the bloodstream and then transported to cells throughout the body for energy, growth, and repair.

The remaining undigested food passes into the large intestine, where water is absorbed, and the remaining waste is formed into stool, which is eventually excreted from the body. This intricate process ensures that our bodies have the necessary components to function properly and maintain health.

Here are some facts about eating and digestion:

- → The average stomach can hold around 4 pounds of food.
- → Digestion begins in the mouth, where enzymes in saliva start breaking down food. An average person produces two pints of saliva per day.
- → The average human stomach can hold about 1–1.5 liters of food and liquid.
- → The stomach produces gastric acid (hydrochloric acid) to aid in digestion and kill harmful bacteria, and it is so strong that it can even dissolve nails!

- The small intestine is where most digestion and nutrient absorption occurs, measuring about 20 feet in length.
- The large intestine is 5 feet in length.
- You produce an average of 3–8 ounces of poop per day.
- The liver produces approximately 27–34 fluid ounces of bile per day, which is essential for breaking down fat in the foods we eat.
- Food takes approximately 6–8 hours to pass through the stomach and small intestine.
- The large intestine absorbs water to transform any food that can't be digested into waste.
- Chewing food thoroughly breaks down food into smaller pieces. This makes digestion easier! Remember that when you eat next!
- Eating slowly and mindfully makes it easier to digest food and reduces the likelihood of getting a tummy ache. Chewing food 20–40 times is ideal.
- Food takes about 20 minutes to reach your stomach and can spend as long as 4 hours there.
- When you drink a can of soda or eat too fast, you burp because you've ingested too much air.
- It smells bad when you fart because it is air mixed with fermented bacteria.
- The body takes about 24–72 hours to completely digest food from start to finish.
- Staying hydrated is essential for healthy digestion, as water helps break down food and absorb nutrients. In fact, your poop is about 75% water!

Surprising Facts

The stomach has its own set of neurons, known as the enteric nervous system, which means it can communicate with the brain independently to some extent, influencing feelings of hunger and fullness.

The stomach has a protective lining that regenerates itself every few days to prevent the organ from digesting itself due to the acidic environment created by gastric juices.

Chapter Three

Marvelous Marvels of Nature

Nature is full of incredible wonders, and in this chapter, we dive into some of its most fascinating aspects. From the tiny plants that can heal us to the towering mountains shaping our landscapes, nature's marvels are all around us. Have you ever thought about how plants make their food or how animals survive in extreme conditions? There's so much hidden magic in the natural world waiting to be discovered.

In this chapter, we'll explore the amazing power and beauty of nature through various lenses. Get ready to be amazed by the endless marvels that Mother Nature offers!

Plant Power

Plants are truly amazing when you think about it. They do so many incredible things that we may not always notice, but they're essential for our planet's health and survival. Plants possess a variety of remarkable powers that play crucial roles in their survival and the ecosystem:

- → **Photosynthesis:** Plants convert sunlight into energy, producing oxygen and glucose, which are essential for life on Earth.
- → **Healing properties:** Many plants contain medicinal compounds that can heal ailments, reduce inflammation, and promote overall health.
- → **Air purification:** Plants can filter pollutants from the air, improving air quality.
- → **Soil stabilization:** Their roots help prevent soil erosion, maintaining the integrity of ecosystems.
- → **Carbon sequestration:** Plants absorb carbon dioxide from the atmosphere, helping to combat climate change.
- → **Habitat creation:** Plants provide habitat and food for various organisms, supporting biodiversity.
- → **Water regulation:** Through transpiration, plants help regulate the water cycle, affecting local and global climates.
- → **Resistance to disease:** Some plants have natural defenses against pests and diseases, making them essential in agricultural practices.
- → **Aesthetic and psychological benefits:** The presence of plants in environments can improve mental well-being and boost creativity.

These powers make plants essential contributors to life on Earth and vital allies in ecological balance.

Let's dive into some of the remarkable abilities and roles of plants in nature:

- → Plants make up about 80% of the Earth's biomass.
- → There are over 390,000 known plant species in the world.

- The tallest tree in the world is a coastal redwood named Hyperion, measuring about 379.7 feet tall.
- Bamboo is the fastest-growing plant on Earth, with some species growing up to 35 inches in a single day.
- Some plants can live for thousands of years; for example, the bristlecone pine can live for over 5,000 years.
- Venus flytraps are carnivorous plants that can snap shut to capture insects for nutrients.
- About 90% of the food humans eat comes from just 30 plants.
- The giant water lily can have leaves that measure up to 10 feet in diameter.
- There are more than 400 billion trees in the Amazon rainforest alone.
- Cacti can store water for long periods, allowing them to survive in arid environments.
- The world's oldest living plant is a clonal colony of quaking aspen trees in Utah, known as Pando, estimated to be around 80,000 years old.
- Some plants, like the rubber tree, produce latex, which can be harvested for rubber products.
- Mangroves are unique plants that can thrive in salty coastal environments and play a crucial role in protecting shorelines.
- Plants can "sleep" at night by closing their leaves, a phenomenon known as nyctinasty.
- The largest flower in the world belongs to the *Rafflesia arnoldii*, which can grow up to 3 feet in diameter.

→ Photosynthesis occurs primarily in the leaves, specifically in the chloroplasts containing chlorophyll. It is chlorophyll that makes them green.

→ Many plants can regenerate; for instance, some can grow back from just a single leaf or stem. For instance, trees can regenerate new buds if branches are cut from their trunks.

→ The Amazon rainforest produces about 20% of the world's oxygen supply.

→ Carnivorous plants, like sundews and pitcher plants, primarily grow in nutrient-poor soils.

→ The process of a plant growing toward light is called phototropism.

Surprising Facts

Some plants can communicate with each other through a network of fungi in the soil, known as the "wood wide web." This symbiotic relationship allows them to share nutrients and warn each other of pests or environmental threats.

The world's largest living organism is a fungus in Oregon's Malheur National Forest that covers an area of nearly 2,385 acres and is estimated to be thousands of years old, showcasing the incredible potential of some fungi.

Geographic Gems

Earth's geography is fascinating for many reasons. From towering mountains to vast deserts, lush forests to intricate coastlines, Earth offers a stunning variety of landscapes, each with unique ecosystems. Natural wonders like the Grand Canyon, the Great Barrier Reef, and Mount Everest showcase the planet's geological and biological diversity. The earth is constantly changing due to natural processes such as erosion, tectonic activity, and climatic shifts, which create new landscapes over time. Geography has influenced historical events, trade routes, and even the rise and fall of civilizations. These aspects make Earth a rich and ever-changing world to explore and study!

Here are some facts about Earth's geographic gems:

- Earth is the third planet from the Sun and the only known planet to support life.
- About 71% of Earth's surface is covered by water, primarily in oceans.
- Mount Everest, located in the Himalayas, is the highest point on Earth, reaching 29,029 feet above sea level.
- The Pacific Ocean is the largest and deepest ocean, covering more than 63 million square miles.
- The Earth's circumference at the equator is about 24,901 miles.
- The Sahara Desert in Africa is the largest hot desert in the world, covering over 3 million square miles.
- Antarctica is the driest, windiest, and coldest continent, holding about 70% of the world's freshwater.
- The Great Rift Valley in East Africa is a major geological

- fault, and at 4,000 miles long and an average width of 30–40 miles, it is one of the largest rift valleys in the world.
- At 3,977 miles, the Amazon River is the largest river, spanning several South American countries.
- The Himalayas include many of the world's tallest mountains. The range is 1,550 miles long.
- At about 133,000 miles, the Great Barrier Reef off the coast of Australia is the largest coral reef system in the world.
- The Nile River is commonly known as the longest river in the world, flowing over 4,135 miles.
- The Earth's landmass is divided into seven continents: Asia, Africa, North America, South America, Antarctica, Europe, and Australia.
- The Pacific Ring of Fire is a horseshoe-shaped zone in the Pacific Ocean basin. Most of the world's earthquakes take place in this area.
- The Amazon Rainforest is home to an incredible diversity of wildlife, with about 3 million species, including 2,500 species of trees.
- The Dead Sea is the lowest point on Earth's surface, lying at approximately 1,410 feet below sea level.
- At 1,904 square miles, the Grand Canyon in the United States is one of the largest and most visited canyons in the world.
- The Mediterranean Sea spans across Europe, Asia, and Africa. It covers an area of 970,000 square miles over 3,000 islands.
- Iceland has lots of volcanic activity because it is located on a geological hotspot on the Mid-Atlantic Ridge.

→ Mount Kilimanjaro in Tanzania is the highest peak in Africa, standing at 19,341 feet above sea level.

> **Surprising Facts**
>
> Russia is so large that it spans 11 time zones, making it the country with the most time zones in the world.
>
> Canada has more lakes than the rest of the world combined, with approximately 2 million lakes covering about 9% of its total area.

Weather Wonders

Weather is fascinating because it constantly changes and influences our daily lives. It can create stunning natural phenomena, such as rainbows and thunderstorms, and plays a crucial role in shaping ecosystems. Weather patterns also reflect the Earth's climate systems and can affect human activities, from agriculture to travel. Additionally, the science of meteorology combines technology and nature, allowing us to predict weather and understand atmospheric conditions.

Here are some wondrous facts about the weather:

→ Lightning can strike the same place multiple times, with some structures being hit hundreds of times during a storm.

→ The world's highest recorded temperature was 134 °F (56.7 °C) in Furnace Creek Ranch, California, in 1913.

→ The largest snowfall recorded in a single storm was 66 inches in Mount Baker, Washington, in 1998.

- Tornadoes can have winds exceeding 300 miles per hour, making them one of the most violent natural disasters.
- The coldest temperature ever recorded on Earth was -128.6 °F (-89.2 °C) in Antarctica in 1983.
- A single hurricane can produce enough energy to power the entire world for a year.
- The average cumulonimbus cloud weighs around a million pounds (or about as much as 100 elephants).
- Rainbows are actually full circles; we typically only see the top half.
- The area known as "Tornado Alley" in the United States experiences an average of 1,000 tornadoes each year, primarily in the spring months.
- Hail can fall at speeds of up to 100 miles per hour, depending on its size and weight.
- The jet stream, a high-altitude wind current 4–8 miles above the Earth's surface, significantly influences weather patterns across the globe.
- Wind chill can make temperatures feel as much as 50 °F colder than the actual temperature.
- There are approximately 40,000 lightning strikes per minute worldwide.
- The ocean generates about 70% of the moisture in our atmosphere, which is crucial for precipitation (liquid or frozen water that forms in the atmosphere and falls back to Earth).
- The term "greenhouse effect" refers to the process of greenhouse gases trapping heat in the Earth's atmosphere, impacting global temperatures.

- Fog can reduce visibility to less than 0.06 miles, making driving extremely hazardous.
- Meteorologists use radar and satellite technology to predict weather and storms.
- A type of cloud, the "mammatus," can indicate severe weather is on the way. These clouds got their name from the Latin word *mamma* meaning "udder."
- The Atacama Desert in South America is the driest place on Earth; some parts of it have never seen rain!
- Mawsynram in India is the wettest place on Earth. On average, it receives 467 inches of rain per year. In 1985, it broke its record with 1,000 inches of rain recorded for that year alone!

Surprising Facts

There are 14.6 million thunderstorms each year, and 40,000 take place in various parts of the world every day!

Did you know that in some parts of the world, it can rain fish? This phenomenon, known as "animal rain," occurs when strong winds lift small animals such as fish or frogs into the atmosphere, which then fall back to the ground with precipitation.

Underwater World

The underwater world is a mesmerizing realm filled with diverse ecosystems, vibrant marine life, and stunning landscapes. It encompasses everything from coral reefs teeming with color to deep-sea trenches that hold mysteries yet to be uncovered.

In this aquatic paradise, you'll find a myriad of creatures, including schools of fish, graceful dolphins, majestic whales, and intricate coral formations. The interplay of light and water creates breathtaking visuals, while the sounds of the ocean add a serene soundtrack to the experience.

Exploring the underwater world can reveal the wonders of biodiversity, the delicate balance of ecosystems, and the importance of conservation efforts to protect these habitats from pollution, climate change, and human activity. It's a fascinating and essential part of our planet that continues to inspire curiosity and awe.

Here are some fascinating facts about the underwater world:

- → The world's longest chain of mountains is in the ocean. The mid-ocean ridge is almost entirely underneath the ocean and stretches across a distance of 40,389 miles. This mountain chain has been less explored than the surface of Mars or Venus!
- → There are more historic artifacts under the sea than there are in all the world's museums. Did you know that around 1,000 shipwrecks lie off the Florida Keys alone?
- → It is believed that between 70 and 80% of the oxygen we breathe is produced by marine plants, most of which are marine algae.

- You can find rivers and lakes beneath the ocean because when salt water combines with hydrogen sulfide, it becomes denser than the rest of the water around it, enabling it to form a river or lake that flows under the sea.
- About 50% of the United States exists under the sea.
- The pressure in the deep ocean can be over 1,000 times the standard atmospheric pressure at sea level.
- The world's largest ocean, the Pacific Ocean, contains around 25,000 islands.
- Jellyfish have been around for over 500 million years, making them one of the oldest living creatures on Earth.
- The ocean helps stabilize the Earth's climate by absorbing 30% of our emissions of carbon dioxide.
- Most bony fish have more than one set of nostrils. Unlike other mammals, the nostrils of fish do not open in the back of their mouth and are not used for breathing. They are used for smelling. Fish need a strong sense of smell to detect the presence of food in the water, hence the need for two sets of nostrils!
- The ocean's currents spread heat around the planet, affecting weather patterns. The Antarctic Circumpolar Current is the most powerful.
- Overfishing can lead to some fish becoming extinct, and it is now impossible to fish in some areas.
- There are underwater caves that have been discovered and explored but have not been properly studied. The longest known underwater cave is Sistema Sac Actun in Mexico, which is 216 miles long!
- The average depth of the ocean is about 12,080 feet.

- Hydrothermal vents on the ocean floor are home to unique ecosystems that depend on bacteria to create new life rather than photosynthesis because there is no light.
- Many marine animals, such as octopuses and cuttlefish, can change color to camouflage themselves from predators.
- The ocean is home to many different plants and creatures including coral reefs, kelp forests, deep-sea trenches, and abyssal plains.

Surprising Facts

The ocean is home to "brine pools," which are deep underwater lakes filled with highly saline water. These pools are so concentrated that they create a distinct boundary, effectively acting like a liquid barrier that prevents light from penetrating and supports unique ecosystems.

Many underwater creatures, like octopuses and squids, can change the color and texture of their skin in a matter of seconds to blend in with their surroundings, communicate, or even express their moods! This remarkable ability, known as adaptive coloration, is made possible by special cells in their skin called chromatophores.

Natural Disasters

Natural disasters are catastrophic events that occur as a result of natural processes of the Earth. They can take various forms, including:

- **Earthquakes:** These are sudden shaking of the ground due to tectonic plate movements.
- **Tsunamis:** These are large ocean waves caused by underwater earthquakes or volcanic eruptions.
- **Hurricanes, typhoons, or cyclones:** These are powerful tropical storms with strong winds and heavy rain.
- **Floods:** These are the overflow of water onto normally dry land, often caused by heavy rain or melting snow.
- **Wildfires:** These are uncontrolled fires that spread rapidly through vegetation.
- **Volcanic eruptions:** These are the explosive release of magma, gases, and ash from volcanoes.
- **Tornadoes:** These are violently rotating columns of air extending from thunderstorms to the ground.
- **Landslides:** These are sudden and fast movement of rock and earth down a slope, often triggered by heavy rainfall.

These events can have devastating impacts on communities, infrastructure, and the environment, often leading to loss of life and significant economic damage. Preparedness and response strategies are crucial in mitigating the effects of natural disasters.

Here are some facts about natural disasters:

- Earthquakes are caused by the movement of tectonic plates and can occur anywhere, though they are most frequent at plate boundaries.

→ The world's biggest tidal wave was over 1,720 feet tall and was spotted at Lituya Bay, Alaska. That's 500 feet taller than the Empire State Building!

→ The deadliest earthquake in recorded history occurred in Shaanxi, China, in 1556, killing approximately 830,000 people.

→ Hurricanes can produce winds of over 157 miles per hour and can cause serious flooding and damage.

→ Tsunamis are often triggered by underwater earthquakes and can travel across entire ocean basins, striking coastlines with little warning. Waves can travel at speeds of up to 500 miles per hour.

→ Floods are the result of heavy rainfall, storm surges, melting snow, or dam breaches and cause more damage than any other natural disaster. About 90% of all natural disasters involve flooding.

→ Tornadoes form from severe thunderstorms and can produce winds exceeding 300 miles per hour, resulting in widespread destruction.

→ Volcanic eruptions can expel ash, gas, and lava, leading to loss of life and significant changes in the environment. Lava can reach temperatures of 1,300–2,200 °F.

→ The word "volcano" comes from the Latin *Vulcan*, the Roman god of fire.

→ Wildfires are either the result of natural causes, such as lightning, or human activities. Up to 89% of wildfires are caused by humans. They are more likely to happen in dry conditions or there are strong winds. Wildfires can move at speeds of up to 14 miles per hour.

→ Earthquakes are measured with a seismograph.

- The largest hailstone ever found in the United States was over 7 inches in diameter and weighed almost 2 pounds!
- The 2004 Indian Ocean tsunami was one of the deadliest natural disasters in history, claiming over 230,000 lives across 14 countries.
- The Richter scale measures the magnitude of an earthquake. A magnitude 4 earthquake is 10 times stronger than a magnitude 3.
- The hypocenter is the point at the center of an earthquake. About half a million earthquakes are detected every year.
- The 1931 China floods are considered the deadliest natural disaster of the 20th century, resulting in millions of deaths.
- Hurricanes, typhoons, and cyclones are all the same thing. They are given different names depending on where they form in the world. Hurricanes form in the Caribbean Sea and Atlantic Ocean, while typhoons form in the Northwest Pacific and cyclones in the Indian Ocean and South Pacific.
- The term "natural hazard" refers to whether natural disasters are likely to take place, while "natural disaster" refers to the event's impact.
- The word "tsunami" comes from the Japanese words *tsu* meaning "harbor" and *nami* meaning "wave."
- About 90% of the world's earthquakes happen along the Pacific Ring of Fire.
- Recovery from natural disasters can take years or even decades, depending on the severity of the event and the resilience of the affected community.

Surprising Facts

Earthquakes can create "liquid" ground, leading to a phenomenon called liquefaction, where solid ground temporarily behaves like a liquid due to intense shaking.

The deadliest natural disaster in recorded history was the Tangshan earthquake in China in 1976, which killed an estimated 242,000 people.

Would you rather

→ live in "Tornado Alley" or the Pacific Ring of Fire?

→ discover a new power source from plants or water?

→ live in the jungle or live underwater?

Quiz

- ☐ What percentage of the ocean is unexplored and unmapped?
- ☐ What is the phenomenon called when plants "sleep" by closing their leaves at night?
- ☐ What is the largest hot desert in the world?
- ☐ Which ocean is the largest and deepest?
- ☐ Which continent holds about 70% of the world's freshwater?
- ☐ How many lightning strikes occur around the world every minute?
- ☐ How much of the oxygen we breathe is produced by marine plants?
- ☐ What remarkable ability do octopuses and squids have that helps them blend into their surroundings?
- ☐ What causes earthquakes, and where are they most likely to occur?
- ☐ What is the difference between a hurricane, a typhoon, and a cyclone?

Chapter Four

Astounding Astronomy and Sensational Space

Exploring space is like opening a treasure chest of mysteries waiting to be discovered. The universe is filled with incredible sights and phenomena that are hard to imagine from our little corner on Earth. In this chapter, we'll dive into the fascinating world of astronomy and space exploration, where each discovery leads to even more questions. From the planets in our solar system to distant galaxies and cutting-edge technology, there's so much to learn and wonder about.

The Solar System

Our solar system is an amazing and complex place, filled with various celestial objects that together create a cosmic neighborhood. At the center of it all is the Sun, a massive ball of burning gas that provides light and heat to everything else. The Sun's gravity holds the solar system together, keeping planets, dwarf planets, moons, asteroids, and comets in their orbits.

Here are some interesting facts about the solar system:

- The solar system is about 4.6 billion years old.
- It consists of the Sun, eight planets, their moons, and other celestial bodies.
- Mercury is the closest planet to the Sun. A year lasts 88 Earth days.
- Venus is the hottest planet, with surface temperatures over 900 °F (475 °C).
- Earth is the only planet known to support life.
- The Earth is 93 million miles away from the sun. We are orbiting the sun at 67,000 miles per hour!
- Mars is often called the "Red Planet" due to its iron oxide-rich surface. Did you know that a year on Mars is 687 Earth days long?
- Jupiter is the largest planet in the solar system, more than 11 times the diameter of Earth.
- Saturn is famous for its stunning ring system made of ice and rock particles. A year on Saturn is 29.4 Earth years!
- A day on Uranus is 17 hours long but it takes 84 Earth years to orbit the sun.
- Neptune is known for its deep blue color and strong winds, the fastest in the solar system, reaching speeds of up to 1,200 miles per hour!
- Neptune is 2.78 billion miles away from the Sun.
- The asteroid belt between Mars and Jupiter contains millions of asteroids.

- The Earth is the only planet with an approximately 24-hour day.
- Jupiter has the shortest day of all the planets, as a day on Jupiter lasts only 9 hours and 55 minutes.
- Venus has the longest days, with one Venus day lasting 243 Earth days!
- Pluto was reclassified as a dwarf planet in 2006 by the International Astronomical Union.
- There are five recognized dwarf planets: Pluto, Eris, Haumea, Makemake, and Ceres.
- The Kuiper Belt is a region beyond Neptune filled with icy bodies and dwarf planets like Pluto.
- Oort Cloud is a theoretical cloud of ice and dust that is believed to surround the solar system.
- The Sun contains over 99% of the entire solar system's mass.
- Light from the Sun takes about 8 minutes and 20 seconds to reach Earth.
- There are more than 200 moons in the solar system.
- Ganymede, a moon of Jupiter, is larger than the planet Mercury.
- The Great Red Spot on Jupiter is a giant storm that has raged for over 350 years.
- Saturn's moon, Titan, has a dense atmosphere and is known for its methane lakes.
- Earth's atmosphere protects us from solar and cosmic radiation.

- In 1929, Edwin Hubble discovered that the universe was expanding. His discovery changed the way scientists viewed the universe. Before this, many believed that the universe was static and unchanging. However, Hubble demonstrated that galaxies are moving away from each other, suggesting that the universe is growing larger over time.
- Blue stars are hotter and more massive than red stars, burning their fuel quickly. One of the hottest blue stars has a temperature of 90,000 °F!
- The sun is classified as a G-type main sequence star (or G dwarf).
- Pulsars are highly magnetized rotating neutron stars that emit beams of electromagnetic radiation. They measure only 12 miles in diameter.
- The largest known star, UY Scuti, is about 1,700 times larger than the sun.
- Dark matter is an elusive substance that makes up about 27% of the universe's mass-energy content.
- Galaxy clusters can contain hundreds or thousands of galaxies bound together by gravity.
- The parts of the universe that are seen and known to us, as much as still to be discovered, are about 93 billion light-years in diameter.
- Stars spend most of their lives in the main sequence phase of their life cycle. It took the sun 20 million years to form, but it has spent 10 billion years in its main life cycle.
- A star's life cycle begins with a nebula, followed by a protostar, and then progresses into the main sequence. After that, it turns into a red giant, which may lead to a

supernova, before finally becoming either a black hole or a white dwarf depending on its mass. This cycle can take billions of years, and the materials ejected during the death of stars contribute to the formation of new stars, continuing the cycle.

- A supernova is a powerful explosion that occurs at the end of a star's life cycle.
- The Crab Nebula is the remnant of a supernova that was observed in 1054 A.D.
- Supermassive black holes are found at the centers of most galaxies, including the Milky Way.
- The cosmic microwave background (CMB) radiation is the afterglow of the Big Bang, filling the universe with a faint microwave signal. It is a form of electromagnetic radiation that is almost uniform in all directions and represents the oldest light in the universe, dating back to about 380,000 years after the Big Bang when the universe cooled enough for atoms to form and photons to travel freely. The CMB provides crucial evidence for the Big Bang theory and offers insights into the early conditions of the universe.
- Quasars are extremely luminous objects powered by black holes at the centers of distant galaxies.
- The Hubble Space Telescope has helped astronomers discover the age and expansion rate of the universe. The universe is 13.8 billion years old. This was discovered by a space telescope that travels at 17,500 miles per hour.

> **Surprising Facts**
>
> Some stars can be so massive that they end their life cycles in spectacular supernova explosions, becoming black holes, while others may shed their outer layers and turn into beautiful planetary nebulae.
>
> Galaxies are not static; they can collide and merge with one another, which can lead to the formation of new stars as the gas and dust from both galaxies interact. This process can result in the creation of entirely new galaxies over millions of years.

Space Exploration

Space exploration is the investigation of outer space through the use of science and technology. It includes a wide range of activities, from sending robotic spacecraft to study distant planets and moons to sending humans to the International Space Station (ISS) and beyond.

Space exploration continues to capture human imagination and advance our understanding of the universe.

Here are some interesting facts about space exploration:

- → The first artificial satellite, Sputnik 1, was launched by the Soviet Union in 1957.
- → In 1961, Yuri Gagarin became the first human to travel into space.
- → NASA's Apollo 11 mission in 1969 successfully landed the first humans on the Moon.
- → The Mars Exploration Rover program has been exploring

the surface of Mars since 1997, with rovers like Spirit, Opportunity, Curiosity, and Perseverance.

→ The ISS has been continuously inhabited since November 2000.

→ The Voyager 1 spacecraft, launched in 1977, is the farthest human-made object from Earth.

→ The first woman in space was Valentina Tereshkova, who flew on Vostok 6 in 1963.

→ The Kepler space telescope, operational from 2009 to 2018, discovered thousands of exoplanets.

→ SpaceX's Falcon 9 became the first privately developed rocket to reach orbit in 2010.

→ The distance from Earth to the Moon is approximately 238,855 miles.

→ The Sun accounts for about 99.86% of the mass in our solar system.

→ The first crewed mission to Mars is planned for the 2030s by NASA. Right now, they are doing simulations on Earth.

→ The Perseverance rover is searching for signs of ancient life on Mars and collecting samples for future return to Earth.

→ The first spacewalk was performed by Alexei Leonov in 1965.

→ Jupiter's moon Europa is believed to have a subsurface ocean beneath its icy crust, making it a candidate for extraterrestrial life.

→ The largest volcano in the solar system is Olympus Mons on Mars, standing about 13.6 miles high.

→ Uranus spins sideways as its axis is tilted by over 90 degrees, which causes it to spin backward. This is because it collided with another planet billions of years ago.

→ More than 2,000 satellites are orbiting Earth.

→ The first successful animal in space was a dog named Laika, launched aboard Sputnik 2 on November 3, 1957.

→ The Lunar Module used during Apollo missions was designed to land on the Moon and return astronauts to the command module.

→ Mars's atmosphere is 95% carbon dioxide, making it inhospitable for humans.

→ The Apollo missions returned 842 pounds of lunar rock and soil to Earth.

→ The Space Shuttle program ran from 1981 to 2011 and completed 135 missions.

→ Light takes about 8 minutes and 20 seconds to travel from the Sun to Earth.

→ Some scientists believe that there are approximately half a million bits of space junk floating around the universe!

Surprising Facts

There are more stars in the universe than there are grains of sand on all the beaches on Earth. It's estimated that there are over 100 billion galaxies, each containing millions or even billions of stars.

Did you know that astronauts on the ISS experience about 15 sunrises and sunsets every day? It's true! It's because the ISS orbits Earth approximately every 90 minutes.

Everyday Innovations

Technologies developed for space exploration have practical applications on Earth. Memory foam, initially created for NASA's spacecraft seats to improve crash protection, is now used in mattresses and pillows, enhancing comfort and sleep quality for millions. Cordless tools, designed for astronauts to work in space without the inconvenience of cords, are now everyday household items, making tasks easier and more efficient. Freeze-dried food, essential for long missions due to its lightweight and long shelf life, is popular among campers and hikers today, providing convenient, nutritious meal options.

Here are some facts about the practical applications of technologies developed for space exploration that have been successfully used on Earth:

- Satellite imagery is used for weather forecasting and environmental monitoring.
- GPS technology, originally developed for military navigation, is now essential for civilian use in smartphones and vehicles.
- Water purification systems from space missions are used in disaster relief and remote areas.
- Advanced materials developed for space suits such as nylon and spandex are now used in sports equipment and safety gear.
- Robotics technology from space exploration has found applications in medical surgery and rehabilitation.
- Thermoregulation materials used in space are now used in clothing and home insulation.

- Techniques developed for isolating pathogens in space are applied in food safety and disease detection.
- Aerospace technology contributes to the development of efficient energy solutions, including solar power systems.
- Imaging sensors developed for Mars rovers are used in autonomous vehicles and drones.
- Communication satellite technology enhances global telecommunication networks and broadband access.
- 3D printing technologies for building spacecraft are now being used in construction and manufacturing.
- Virtual reality and augmented reality technologies from astronaut training are now used in education and training.
- Innovations in battery technology for space vehicles have led to improved electric vehicle performances.
- The development of lightweight materials for spacecraft is now used in the automotive and aerospace industries for fuel efficiency.
- Techniques for detecting gas leaks from space are now used in monitoring environmental pollution.
- Space weather technology helps protect power grids and communications systems from solar storms.
- Knowledge gained from studying cosmic radiation contributes to cancer treatment and radiation therapy methods.
- Analyzing soil samples in space has led to advancements in agriculture and soil conservation techniques.
- Spacecraft navigation systems improve the precision of various Earth-based industries, including agriculture.

- Remote sensing technology helps in urban planning and land use management.
- The design and engineering processes used in spacecraft contribute to the development of innovative consumer products.
- Heat-resistant materials developed for space vehicles are utilized in fireproof clothing and equipment.
- Technologies for recycling air and water in spacecraft are used in sustainable living solutions on Earth.
- Satellite monitoring aids disaster response and climate change adaptation strategies.
- Medical imaging technologies refined by space missions are used in advanced diagnostic equipment like MRIs.

Surprising Facts

Memory foam: Originally developed by NASA in the 1960s to improve the safety of aircraft cushions, memory foam has become a popular material in mattresses, pillows, and other comfort products. Its ability to conform to the body and distribute weight evenly makes it a staple in the bedding industry.

Satellite navigation systems: While most people associate GPS with driving directions, the technology originally developed for military applications in satellite navigation has transformed numerous aspects of daily life. It is used for everything from tracking fitness activities with smartwatches to food delivery apps, optimizing routes for efficiency.

Would you rather

→ go and stay on Venus (the hottest planet, with surface temperatures over 900 °F) or Saturn with its cold temperatures and ice rings?

→ meet the first man (Yuri Gagarin) or the first dog (Laika) to enter space?

→ meet any life-forms that have lived on Mars or Jupiter's moon Europa?

Quiz

- ☐ Which planet is known for having the most powerful magnetic field in the solar system?
- ☐ What is the hottest planet in the solar system?
- ☐ How long does it take for light from the Sun to reach Earth?
- ☐ After our Sun, what is the closest star to Earth, and how far away is it?
- ☐ What happens to a massive star when it collapses under its own gravity?
- ☐ Which galaxy is the nearest spiral galaxy to the Milky Way?
- ☐ What was the name of the first artificial satellite launched by the Soviet Union in 1957?
- ☐ Which mission successfully landed the first humans on the Moon in 1969?
- ☐ Which planet's moon, Europa, is believed to have a subsurface ocean that could harbor life?
- ☐ What technology originally developed for military navigation is now essential for smartphones and vehicles?

Chapter Five

Phenomenal Physical Forces

Phenomenal physical forces shape our universe in seen and unseen ways, affecting everything from the smallest particles to the largest cosmic structures. Did you know gravity is one of the main forces of nature? Have you ever wondered what keeps planets in orbit or why objects fall to the ground? These are all results of the fundamental forces that govern the natural world around us. Understanding these forces can help us grasp how everything fits together, from everyday activities like riding a roller coaster to the mysteries of space like black holes.

Get ready to uncover the secrets behind these amazing forces and their incredible impacts on our lives and the universe!

Gravity

Gravity is one of the most important forces in our universe. Understanding gravity helps us make sense of the world around us and the vast cosmos beyond. Gravity is a force that pulls objects toward each other. Every object with mass has gravity, and the bigger the mass, the stronger the gravitational pull. For example, Earth's gravity keeps us anchored to the ground and makes it possible for us to walk, run, and play without floating away into space.

Here are some interesting facts about gravity:

- → Gravity causes you to shrink throughout the day because gravity compresses our bodies. When we lie down at night, gravity no longer pulls us down, so we get taller!
- → Sir Isaac Newton figured out gravity in 1666 when he saw an apple falling from a tree. It made him wonder what force had propelled it to the ground and why objects like the moon remained in place in the sky. From that, he figured out gravity!
- → The force of gravity depends on the height and weight of the objects and the distance between them.
- → Earth's gravity is approximately 32.2 feet per second squared (ft/s^2) at sea level.
- → Gravity is weaker on the Moon than on Earth, about one sixth as strong.
- → Black holes have such strong gravitational pull that not even light can escape from them.
- → The Sun's gravity keeps the planets in orbit around it. The gravitational pull of the sun at the surface is 899 feet per second squared, which is 27.9 stronger than Earth's gravity!
- → Weight is the measure of the force of gravity acting on an object.
- → The concept of "weightlessness" occurs in free fall conditions, like in orbit.
- → The gravitational force between two objects decreases as the distance between them increases.
- → The term "gravitational field" describes the pull of gravity in a given area.

- Einstein's general theory of relativity describes gravity as the curvature of space-time.
- Gravity affects time; the stronger the gravitational field, the slower time passes.
- Tidal forces from the moon create ocean tides on Earth.
- While gravity pulls objects downward, it is also responsible for the formation of stars and galaxies.
- Objects in space feel weightless because they are in continuous free fall.
- The gravitational constant (G) has a value of approximately 6.674×10^{-11} N(m/kg)^2.
- Gravity was not fully understood until Einstein's theories in the early 20th century, which explained how it influences the creation and orbit of objects in space.
- Gravitational waves are ripples in space-time caused by accelerated masses, detected in 2015.
- The gravitational pull of a planet can affect the trajectory of spacecraft.
- The Earth's gravity is not uniform; it varies slightly in different locations due to topography and density. If you are higher up, like on a mountain, you are further from the Earth's center, so the gravitational pull will be weaker. Gravitational pulls from the sun and moon also create tides!
- Some scientists believe dark matter affects gravity on a cosmic scale.
- The concept of antigravity, as seen in science fiction, does not exist in scientific theory.

→ In a vacuum, all objects fall at the same rate, regardless of their mass.

→ The force of gravity extends infinitely, but its strength diminishes with distance.

Surprising Facts

Gravity isn't constant. While we often think of gravity as a fixed force, it actually varies depending on where you are on Earth. For example, gravity is slightly weaker at the equator than at the poles due to the Earth's shape and rotation.

There is gravity in space: Many people assume that once you leave Earth's atmosphere, you are weightless. However, gravity is still present in space; it decreases with distance from massive objects. That's why astronauts aboard the ISS experience microgravity, not complete weightlessness.

Invisible Forces and Fields

Imagine a world where invisible forces shape everything around us. These unseen forces and fields are critical players in how matter and energy behave. Let's dive into three fascinating types of fields—electric, magnetic, and gravitational fields—and see how they shape our everyday lives.

Here are some intriguing facts about invisible forces and fields:

- → Electric fields are produced by electric charges.
- → The strength of an electric field is measured in volts per meter (V/m).
- → Magnetic fields are produced by moving electric charges (currents) and magnets.
- → The strength of a magnetic field is measured in teslas (T).
- → Gravitational fields are created by objects with mass, exerting a force on other masses.
- → The strength of a gravitational field is measured in newtons per kilogram (N/kg).
- → Electric fields can influence charges, causing them to move and accelerate.
- → Magnetic fields can change the direction of moving charges but do no work on them, as they don't change their speed.
- → Gravitational fields always act to pull objects together; they are always attractive.
- → The concept of electric field lines illustrates the direction and strength of the field, with denser lines indicating stronger fields.

- The Earth's magnetic field protects the planet from harmful solar radiation.
- Gravitational fields diminish with distance, following the inverse square law. This means they get less powerful the further away they are from an object.
- Electric fields can be shielded using conductive materials (materials that absorb electricity).
- Magnetic fields can also be shielded, though it usually requires special materials like mu-metal.
- The relationship between electricity and magnetism is described by Maxwell's equations. Maxwell's equations are a set of four fundamental equations in electromagnetism that describe how electric and magnetic fields interact and propagate.
- Gravitational fields are responsible for keeping planets in orbit around stars.
- The unit of charge, the coulomb, is a measure of electric charge in an electric field.
- The Lorentz force describes the force experienced by a charged particle moving through an electric and magnetic field.
- A changing magnetic field induces an electric current in a conductor, a principle known as electromagnetic induction.
- Superconductors can exhibit perfect diamagnetism, expelling magnetic fields.
- The gravitational field of a planet can be visualized using gravitational field lines, which point toward the center of the mass.
- Electric fields can be stronger than gravitational fields at

small scales, such as those found in atoms.

→ The speed of light in a vacuum is the maximum speed at which information can travel through electric and magnetic fields.

→ Black holes have extremely strong gravitational fields that can warp the fabric of space-time itself.

Surprising Facts

Electric fields can exist in a vacuum, meaning they can exist without any physical charges nearby, while magnetic fields are always generated by moving electric charges or currents, indicating a strong connection between electricity and magnetism.

The Earth's magnetic field is not constant; it undergoes periodic reversals over geological timescales, meaning that the magnetic north and south poles can switch places, an event that occurs approximately every 200,000–300,000 years.

Wonders of Waves in Light, Sound, and Water

Waves are all around us in many different forms. They help us see, hear, and even enjoy a day at the beach. They also appear as light and help sound move so that we can hear what's going on. Let's explore how waves behave and why they are so important.

Here are some wonderful facts about waves in light, sound, and water. These facts provide a glimpse into the fascinating nature of waves in different mediums!

Light Waves

- Light travels at approximately 186,282 miles per second in a vacuum.
- Light is an electromagnetic wave and does not require an object to travel through.
- The visible spectrum of light ranges from approximately 0.4 micrometers (violet) to 0.7 micrometers (red).
- White light is composed of multiple colors, which can be seen in a rainbow.
- The colors of the rainbow are red, orange, yellow, green, blue, indigo, and violet.
- Light waves exhibit both wave-like and particle-like properties (wave–particle duality). This means they both travel invisibly in light and also have a tangible mass.
- The frequency of light waves, which indicates how many there are, determines their color.
- Ultraviolet light has a higher frequency than visible light and can cause sunburn.
- Infrared light has a lower frequency than visible light and is associated with heat.
- Light can be polarized, meaning it merges in a single plane.
- The speed of light is slower in materials like water and glass compared to a vacuum.

Sound Waves

- Sound waves are longitudinal waves (a wave that moves in the same direction as the direction of vibrating particles) that travel through a medium (solid, liquid, or gas).

- The speed of sound varies depending on the medium; it travels fastest in solids.
- Human hearing ranges approximately 20–20,000 hertz.
- Sound waves can reflect, refract, and diffract (mirror, change direction, and spread out) when encountering different surfaces.
- Infrasound refers to sound waves below the human hearing range (below 20 hertz).
- Ultrasound refers to sound waves above the human hearing range (above 20,000 hertz).
- The amplitude (sound volume) of a sound wave determines its loudness.
- Sound waves require a medium to spread; they cannot travel in a vacuum.

Water Waves

- Water waves can be classified into two main types: surface waves and internal waves.
- Surface waves are created by wind blowing across the water's surface.
- The height of a water wave is determined by wind speed, duration, and fetch (distance over water).
- The wavelength of water waves can vary from a few centimeters to hundreds of meters.
- Water waves can change direction, leading to changes in wave direction as they approach shorelines, while capillary waves are small ripples on the water surface caused by wind.

> **Surprising Facts**
>
> The shape of an ocean wave is actually a circular motion. As waves pass through water, the water itself mostly moves up and down in a circular pattern rather than just moving forward.
>
> Sound can be heard in space if it is transmitted through a medium (like an astronaut's suit), but in the vacuum of space itself, sound cannot travel at all.

Shocking: Electricity and Lightning

Electricity is a form of energy resulting from the existence of charged particles, such as electrons or protons. It is used to power a vast range of devices and is generated through various means, including fossil fuels, nuclear energy, and renewable resources like wind and solar.

Lightning, on the other hand, is a natural electrical discharge that occurs during thunderstorms. It results from the buildup of electrical charges in the atmosphere as clouds collide and create static electricity. When the charge becomes strong enough, it is released as a flash of light and heat, creating a lightning bolt that can reach temperatures higher than that of the sun's surface.

Both electricity and lightning are integral to our understanding of energy in nature, with lightning serving as a dramatic reminder of the power of electrical forces.

Here are some shocking facts about electricity and lightning:

- → Lightning is a result of static electricity buildup in clouds.
- → A lightning strike can reach temperatures of around 30,000 °F.

- The speed of lightning is approximately 220,000 miles per hour.
- On average, lightning strikes Earth about 100 times every second.
- The sound of thunder is caused by the rapid expansion of air heated by lightning.
- Static electricity occurs when there is an imbalance of electric charges within or on the surface of a material. This then creates static energy. An example would be how a Van de Graaff generator makes your hair stand on end!
- Benjamin Franklin is famous for his experiments with electricity, including the kite and key experiment. In 1752, during a thunderstorm, Franklin flew a kite made of silk material, which was less likely to break in high winds. He attached a metal key to the string of the kite and held the string with a nonconductive material, like a wooden stick, to avoid direct contact with the electricity. The kite was also equipped with a pointed wire to attract the electric charge from the storm clouds. As the storm approached, Franklin observed that the key became positively charged with the buildup of electrical charge from the storm. When he moved his hand near the key, sparks flew from it, confirming the presence of electrical energy. This demonstrated that both lightning and the electricity produced in the laboratory were the same phenomenon.
- The first practical use of electricity in homes was for lighting, using incandescent bulbs in the 1890s.
- Lightning can strike the same place multiple times, especially tall structures.
- Electric currents can be either direct (DC) or alternating (AC). Direct current flows in a constant direction, while

alternating current changes the direction of charge periodically.
- → Earth itself is an electrical conductor, which allows lightning to reach the ground.
- → Lightning can cause wildfires, damage buildings, and even result in serious injuries.
- → Thomas Edison is credited with inventing the first practical light bulb in 1879.
- → The electric eel can produce electric shocks of up to 600 volts.
- → A lightning bolt only lasts about 30 microseconds on average.
- → The average distance between lightning and thunder is about 3 miles.
- → In the United States, around 30 people are killed by lightning each year.
- → Lightning is more frequent in tropical regions and during summer months.
- → Lightning rods were invented to protect buildings from lightning strikes. Lightning rods are used on the Empire State Building in New York City to protect it from lightning as it stands at 1,454 feet tall and is struck by lightning around 20–25 times each year.
- → Water is a good conductor of electricity, which is why people are advised to stay indoors during thunderstorms.
- → The phenomenon of ball lightning, where glowing, spherical objects appear during thunderstorms, is still not fully understood by scientists.

→ Electric power plants create electricity using various sources, including fossil fuels, nuclear energy, and renewable resources.

→ The first worldwide electrical grid was established in 1882 in New York City.

Surprising Facts

A single bolt of lightning can contain up to one billion volts of electricity, which is enough to power a small town for a day.

The temperature of a lightning bolt can reach up to 50,000 °F, which is 5 times hotter than the surface of the sun.

Would you rather

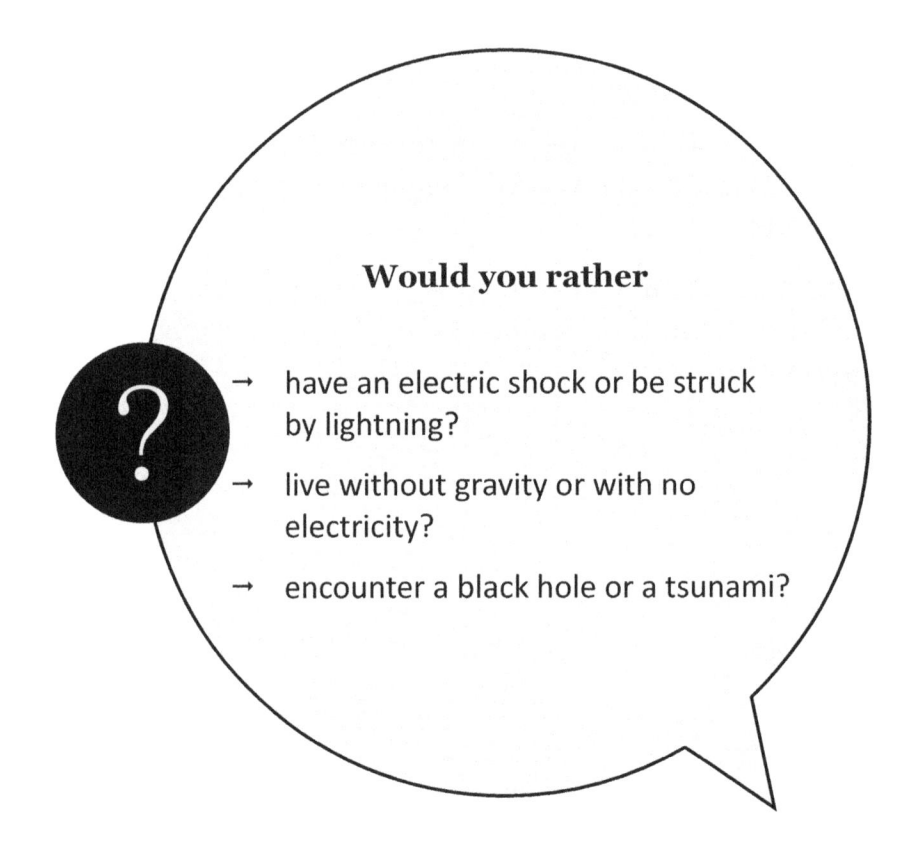

→ have an electric shock or be struck by lightning?

→ live without gravity or with no electricity?

→ encounter a black hole or a tsunami?

Quiz

- ☐ Why do we get taller when we lie down at night?
- ☐ Who discovered gravity, and what made him think about it?
- ☐ What is the strength of an electric field measured in?
- ☐ How does the Earth's magnetic field help protect the planet?
- ☐ What colors make up white light, as seen in a rainbow?
- ☐ What type of light has a higher frequency than visible light and can cause sunburn?
- ☐ How fast does sound travel compared to light in a vacuum?
- ☐ What causes the sound of thunder?
- ☐ How hot can a lightning strike get?
- ☐ Why is it dangerous to be near water during a thunderstorm?

Chapter Six

Inventions That Changed Our World

Exploring the inventions that have changed our world is like going on a treasure hunt through history. From the food we eat to the medicines that keep us healthy, these innovative ideas have shaped the way we live today. Have you ever wondered what life would be like without the refrigerator, or how people used to stay healthy before vaccines? This chapter will take you through some fascinating stories behind everyday objects and groundbreaking discoveries that have made our lives better in countless ways.

Food Inventions

When you think about keeping food fresh and safe to eat, several key innovations have played a significant role. These inventions have changed the way we store, transport, and even produce our food, ensuring that it remains safe, nutritious, and available. Let's dive into some of the breakthroughs in food production and preservation that have had a profound impact on our daily lives.

Here are some facts about food inventions that have significantly influenced our daily lives:

- The refrigerator was invented in 1834 by American Jacob Perkins revolutionizing food preservation.
- Canning was developed in the early 1800s, allowing food to be stored longer and transported easily.
- The microwave oven, introduced by company Raytheon in 1947, transformed cooking times and convenience. However, it was only used for commercial purposes until the 1960s when microwave ovens became affordable and available for home use.
- Instant noodles, invented in Japan by Momofuku Ando of Nissin Foods in 1958, changed quick meal options globally.
- The blender, invented by Stephen J. Poplawski in 1922, made smoothies and soups simpler to prepare.
- The food processor, introduced to the market by Cuisinart in 1973, streamlined meal prep by combining multiple functions.
- Fast-food chains, emerging in the mid-20th century, altered dining culture and convenience. Many believe that the White Castle, which opened in Kansas in 1916, was the first fast-food place in the United States!
- Pasteurization, developed by Louis Pasteur in the 1860s, improved food safety and shelf life.
- The skillet, created for easier stovetop cooking, has been a kitchen staple for centuries.
- Frozen food became accessible in the 1920s, impacting meal prepping and convenience.

- The sandwich, popularized in the 18th century by the Earl of Sandwich, who created it so he could gamble and eat at the same time, revolutionized portable meals.
- The pressure cooker, invented in the 17th century by French physicist Denis Papin, significantly reduced cooking times.
- Processed cheese, developed by Walter Gerber and Fritz Stettler in Switzerland in 1911, has become a staple in many diets.
- The can opener, patented by Ezra J. Warner in 1858, made it easier to access canned goods.
- Nonstick cookware, introduced in the 1960s, changed cooking and cleaning experiences.
- Energy bars, developed in the 1960s, popularized on-the-go nutrition. Back then, they cost between 25 and 50 cents—a bargain!
- The yogurt maker, gaining popularity in the 20th century, encouraged healthier eating habits. Did you know that yogurt was first discovered in Mesopotamia 7,000 years ago?
- The potato chip was invented in 1853, leading to the snacking industry boom.
- The tortilla press, which originated in ancient Mesoamerica and is used for making tortillas, is central to Mexican cuisine.
- The air fryer, emerging in the 2000s and invented by Dutch engineer Fred van der Weij, changed the way people think about frying food.
- The coffee maker, evolving from simple pots to electric

machines, revolutionized beverage preparation. Coffee itself was first drunk in Arabia in the 15th century.

→ Tupperware, invented by Earl Silas Tupper and introduced in the 1940s, transformed food storage and meal prep.

→ The soda can design was perfected in the 1930s, making soft drinks more accessible. That pull tab opening we are all familiar with was invented by Ermal Fraze in 1959.

→ The slow cooker invented by Irving Naxon in 1940, popularized in the 1970s, simplified meal preparation for busy families.

→ Plant-based meat alternatives, emerging in the 21st century, are changing perceptions of meat consumption. In fact, people have actually been eating meat alternatives like tofu for 1,800 years!

Surprising Facts

In 1985, a group of food scientists created a "shortened" version of cornstarch to help create a longer-lasting ice cream which they named ice milk. This invention was a response to providing a healthier alternative that maintained a similar texture and flavor to traditional ice cream.

Did you know that popsicles were invented by accident? It's true! In 1905, 11-year-old Frank Epperson mixed up a sugary soda powder and left it outside on a cold night to freeze, then enjoyed the new frozen treat he had just created the next morning. From that, the popsicle was born!

Medical Inventions

Breakthroughs in medical technology have revolutionized how we treat and diagnose illnesses, significantly improving the quality of life and overall health of people around the world. Four key innovations stand out for their profound impacts: the discovery of antibiotics, the development of vaccines, the introduction of X-ray technology, and advancements in surgical techniques. Each of these breakthroughs has not only saved countless lives but also paved the way for further advancements in medicine.

Here are some fascinating facts about medical inventions:

- Antibiotics were first discovered by Alexander Fleming in 1928 with the accidental discovery of penicillin. The antibiotic was mass-produced during World War II and saved countless lives from bacterial infections.

- The first vaccine was developed by Edward Jenner in 1796 to combat smallpox.

- Vaccines work by stimulating the immune system to recognize and fight against specific pathogens.

- The polio vaccine, developed by Jonas Salk in 1955, dramatically reduced polio incidence worldwide.

- The Bacillus Calmette–Guérin (BCG) vaccine is used to protect against tuberculosis and was developed by Dr. Albert Calmette and Dr. Camille Guérin in 1921 from attenuated strains of the *Mycobacterium*.

- X-rays were discovered by Wilhelm Conrad Röntgen in 1895 while he was experimenting with cathode rays. The first medical use of X-ray technology occurred shortly after its discovery to visualize broken bones.

- Advances in digital imaging technology have made it possible to capture high-quality X-ray images with less radiation.
- The first successful organ transplantation was performed in 1954 with a kidney transplant between identical twins.
- Surgical techniques have evolved significantly with the introduction of minimally invasive procedures, such as laparoscopy, where surgery is performed using small incisions with the aid of a camera.
- Anesthesia, first successfully used in the 19th century, revolutionized surgery by allowing patients to undergo painless procedures. One of the first people to use it was dentist Dr. William Morton in 1846.
- The use of antiseptics in surgery, popularized by Joseph Lister in the 1860s, reduced postoperative infections dramatically.
- The development of robotic surgery systems, like the da Vinci Surgical System, has enhanced precision in complex procedures.
- Telemedicine technology allows for remote consultations, expanding access to surgical expertise in underserved areas like Alaska or islands like Vanuatu.
- The invention of the stethoscope by René Laennec in 1816 provided a new way for doctors to diagnose conditions noninvasively.
- MRI technology, developed by Raymond Damadian in the 1970s, allows for detailed imaging of soft tissues and organs without the use of radiation.
- The development of endoscopy by German doctor Philipp Bozzini in 1806 enabled physicians to view the inside of the gastrointestinal tract through a flexible tube.

- The introduction of laparoscopic surgery has led to shorter recovery times and fewer complications compared to traditional open surgery.

- The accidental invention of the pacemaker by Wilson Greatbatch in the 1950s has helped regulate heart rhythms in patients with arrhythmias, irregular heartbeats that can cause your heart to beat too fast, too slow, or in an irregular rhythm.

- 3D printing technology invented by Chuck Hull in 1986 is being utilized in surgery to create patient-specific implants and models for complex procedures.

- Surgical robots have been used to enhance precision in orthopedic surgeries, leading to better outcomes for joint replacements.

- The WHO developed a global vaccination program to combat infectious diseases, leading to the eradication of smallpox in 1980.

- In 1954, the first successful kidney transplant took place.

Surprising Facts

The first successful blood transfusion was performed in 1667 by Dr. Jean-Baptiste Denis, who used animal blood, specifically from a sheep, to transfuse into a human, marking the beginning of experimentation with transfusions.

The invention of the stethoscope in 1816 by Dr. René Laennec was at first just a wooden tube used to amplify sound, but it has evolved into a sophisticated device that allows doctors to listen to the internal sounds of a patient's body, significantly improving diagnostics.

Science and Engineering Inventions

Significant inventions have had a profound impact on human life, shaping industries, science, and our understanding of the world around us. Some examples include the steam engine, electrical power, telecommunications, and space exploration. All of these inventions have changed our lives for the better. Let's dive into some groundbreaking advancements that have changed our lives forever.

Here are some interesting facts about various science and engineering inventions:

- The wheel invented around 3500 B.C.E. is considered one of the most significant inventions in human history.
- Johannes Gutenberg is credited with inventing the movable type printing press in 1454, which greatly facilitated the spread of literature and ideas.
- Alexander Graham Bell patented the first practical telephone in 1876.
- Thomas Edison is credited with inventing the first commercially practical incandescent light bulb in 1879.
- The airplane, invented by the Wright brothers in 1903, changed the way people travel across the globe.
- James Watt improved the steam engine's efficiency in 1764, contributing significantly to the Industrial Revolution.
- The internet, which emerged in the late 20th century, has transformed communication and information sharing.
- The first computer, ENIAC, was developed in the 1940s and weighed over 27 tons.

- In 1911, Marie Curie was the first woman to win a Nobel Prize, recognized for her work in radioactivity.
- The vacuum cleaner, invented in the 1860s, greatly simplified household cleaning. It was called the Whirlwind and was invented by Ives W. McGaffey.
- The barcode, patented in 1952, has made inventory management and checkout processes more efficient.
- The rechargeable battery was developed in the late 19th century and has since been essential for portable electronics.
- The first successful heart transplant was performed by Dr. Christiaan Barnard in 1967.
- The microscope, invented in the late 16th century, opened up the world of microbiology.
- The GPS technology, developed for military use, is now integral to navigation in everyday life.
- The first synthetic dye, mauveine, was discovered by Sir William Henry Perkin in 1856.
- The safety pin was invented by Walter Hunt in 1849, providing a simple yet effective fastening solution.
- The first solar cell was created in 1954, harnessing the sun's energy for electricity.
- The pacemaker, invented by Paul Zoll in the 1950s, helps regulate heartbeats.
- The automatic transmission in vehicles was developed in the 1930s, enhancing driving convenience.
- The first email was sent by Ray Tomlinson in 1971, marking the beginning of digital communication.

- The concept of flight was inspired by birds, leading to innovations in aerodynamics.
- The electric motor, developed in the early 19th century, paved the way for modern machinery.
- The first space satellite, Sputnik, was launched by the Soviet Union in 1957, initiating the Space Age.

Surprising Facts

The first computer mouse was invented by Douglas Engelbart in 1964, and it was made of wood! The original design used two metal wheels to track movement.

Did you know that when trains were first invented, people thought riding them could cause instant insanity? It's mad but true. It was believed that the sounds and motion of train travel could cause people to go mad, literally (Hayes, 2017).

Quirky Facts About Famous Inventors and Accidental Inventions

The people who have invented some of the most useful and interesting things are fascinating in their own right. Also, accidental inventions have often led to remarkable breakthroughs in various fields. These inventors show that sometimes the best discoveries come when things don't go as planned!

Here are some facts about a few famous inventors and their notable accidental inventions:

- Thomas Edison is credited with inventing the phonograph in 1877, the first device to record and playback sound.
- Alexander Graham Bell, often credited with inventing the telephone, also worked with deaf individuals to develop communication methods.
- Nikola Tesla invented the alternating current electrical system, used in most power systems today.
- The Wright brothers, Orville and Wilbur, are known for inventing the first successful airplane.
- The first successful flight by the Wright brothers took place on December 17, 1903, and lasted for 12 seconds.
- TV dinners were invented by a Swanson salesman named Gerry Thomas in 1953 who had the idea of freezing dinners and placing them on metal trays for convenience.
- Hedy Lamarr, a famous actress, co-invented a frequency-hopping spread spectrum technology, paving the way for modern wireless communication.

- Steve Jobs and Steve Wozniak co-founded Apple Inc. and played a key role in the personal computing revolution.
- Tim Berners-Lee invented the World Wide Web in 1989, fundamentally changing how information is shared globally.
- The invention of the light bulb by Thomas Edison is often mistakenly attributed solely to him; Joseph Swan independently developed a similar bulb, and others also worked on the concept.
- Eli Whitney invented the cotton gin, which revolutionized the production of cotton and had a significant impact on the economy of the Southern United States.
- Marie Van Brittan Brown invented the first home security system in 1966.
- The Post-it note was invented accidentally by Spencer Silver while he was attempting to create a strong adhesive.
- The first practical refrigerator was invented by Carl von Linde in 1876, which transformed food preservation.
- The first bicycle was invented by Karl Drais in 1817, paving the way for modern cycling.
- Barbara McClintock developed the concept of "jumping genes" in genetics, earning a Nobel Prize for her work.
- Lillian Gilbreth, one of the first female engineers, contributed significantly to industrial management and efficiency studies.
- Potato chips were accidentally created when a chef sliced potatoes very thinly and fried them until they were crispy. The customer loved the new dish, and a new snack was born!
- While working on radar technology during World War II,

Percy Spencer noticed that a chocolate bar in his pocket had melted. This led to the invention of the microwave oven.

→ John Gorrie, an early advocate for mechanical refrigeration, invented ice-making machines to cool air for patients. His work laid the groundwork for modern air-conditioning.

→ Not so much an inventor but a writer, William Gibson coined the term "cyberspace" in his novel *Neuromancer*, bringing attention to the concept of virtual reality and influencing real-world technology.

→ Invented as a medicinal tonic, Coca-Cola was accidentally created in 1886 by Dr. John Pemberton when he mixed sugar syrup with carbonated water.

Surprising Facts

Did you know that corn flakes were invented accidentally? It's true. Will and John Kellogg accidently invented corn flakes when they left a pot of boiled grain on the stove for several days. This caused the corn to flake and corn flakes were born!

Velcro is also an accidental invention! When Swiss engineer Georges de Mestral was hiking in 1941, he discovered burrs clinging to his pants and his dog's fur. He noticed that the hooks of the burr would stick to anything loop-shaped. This then gave him the idea for Velcro!

Chapter Challenge

Here we are introducing something new: the chapter challenge.

1. Can you think of an invention you would like to create—something that has never been invented before but you think would be useful? Perhaps you'd get some use of a mechanical hairbrush or an automatic bedmaker?

2. Draw a picture of your invention and write a description of what it does. With any luck, you too could be an inventor one day!

Would you rather

- live in a world where the internet hadn't been invented or one where the wheel didn't exist?
- that potato chips or Coca-Cola had never been invented?
- meet Alexander Graham Bell (the inventor of the telephone) or Marie Curie (the discoverer of radioactivity)?

Quiz

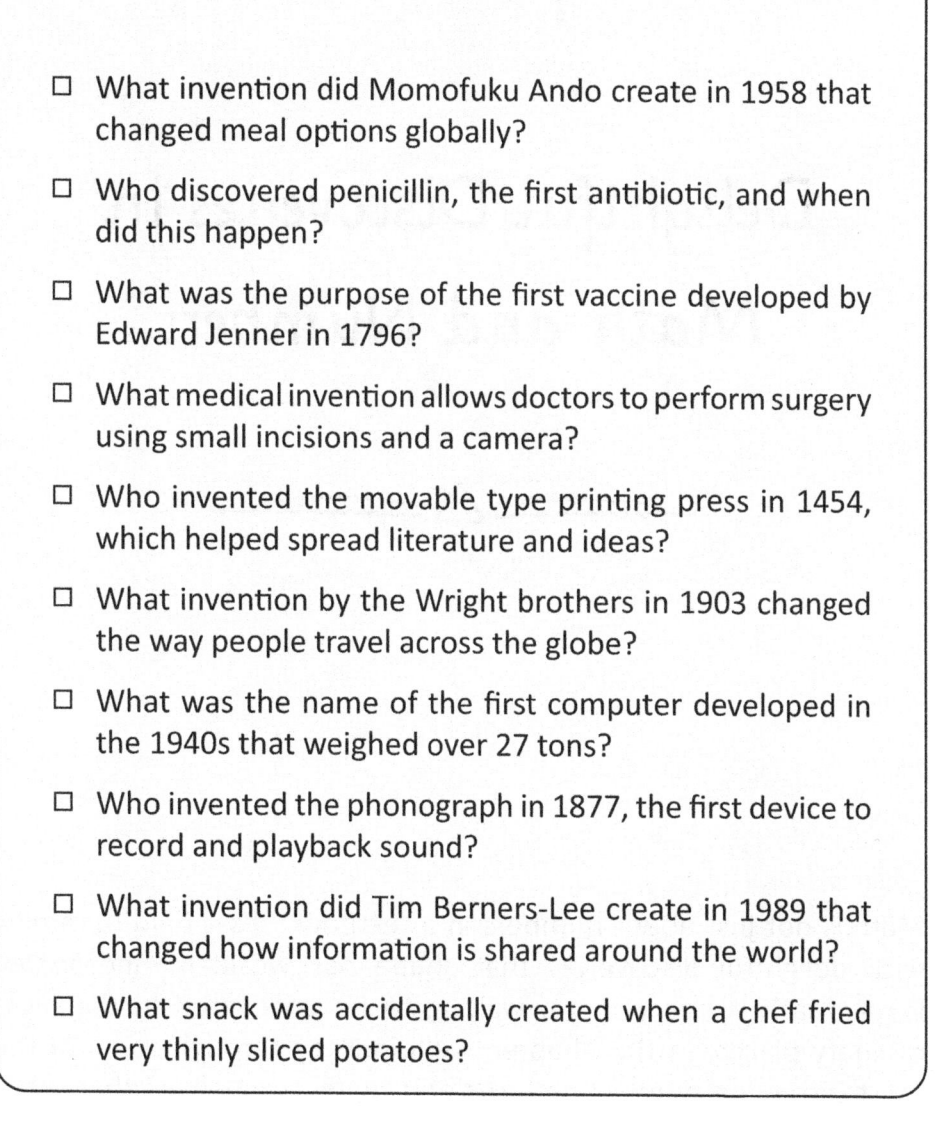

- ☐ What invention did Momofuku Ando create in 1958 that changed meal options globally?
- ☐ Who discovered penicillin, the first antibiotic, and when did this happen?
- ☐ What was the purpose of the first vaccine developed by Edward Jenner in 1796?
- ☐ What medical invention allows doctors to perform surgery using small incisions and a camera?
- ☐ Who invented the movable type printing press in 1454, which helped spread literature and ideas?
- ☐ What invention by the Wright brothers in 1903 changed the way people travel across the globe?
- ☐ What was the name of the first computer developed in the 1940s that weighed over 27 tons?
- ☐ Who invented the phonograph in 1877, the first device to record and playback sound?
- ☐ What invention did Tim Berners-Lee create in 1989 that changed how information is shared around the world?
- ☐ What snack was accidentally created when a chef fried very thinly sliced potatoes?

Chapter Seven

Delightful Discoveries in Math and Numbers

Math is not just about numbers in a textbook; it's a field brimming with delightful discoveries that shape our world in unexpected ways. Math is everywhere, waiting to be uncovered in the most ordinary places. In this chapter, we'll journey through some of the most intriguing number patterns and quirky sequences that make mathematics magical. By the end of this chapter, you'll see how these mathematical concepts are woven into the fabric of our daily lives, enriching our understanding of both numbers and the natural world.

Awesome Number Patterns and Quirky Sequences

One of the most captivating aspects of mathematics is the world of number patterns and sequences. These patterns are not just abstract concepts confined to textbooks; they emerge in nature, art, architecture, and even music.

Let's dive into some facts about these fascinating number patterns and sequences that make math magical:

- Four is the only number with the same number of letters as the number.
- An arithmetic sequence is a series of numbers in which the difference between consecutive terms is constant. On the other hand, the Fibonacci sequence is formed by adding the two previous numbers, beginning with 0 and 1 (0, 1, 1, 2, 3, 5, 8, and so on).
- Geometric sequences have a common ratio between consecutive terms, like 2, 4, 8, and 16 (where each term is multiplied by 2).
- The sequence of prime numbers starts with 2, 3, 5, 7, and 11 and continues indefinitely. A prime number can only be divided by the number one and itself.
- Perfect squares form a pattern (1, 4, 9, 16, 25, and so on), where each term is the square of a whole number.
- Triangular numbers can be represented as dots arranged in an equilateral triangle (1, 3, 6, 10, 15, and so on).
- A palindrome in a number sequence is a number that reads the same forward and backward, like 121 or 1331.
- The Lucas sequence is similar to the Fibonacci sequence but starts with 2 and 1 (2, 1, 3, 4, 7, 11, and so on).
- Infinity is something, endless, boundless, and larger than any natural number. It is denoted by the symbol ∞.
- The golden ratio (ϕ, approximately 1.618) is closely related to the Fibonacci sequence, where the ratio of successive Fibonacci numbers approximates the golden ratio.

Surprising Facts

Did you know that there is a specific sequence for building Lego blocks? It's true! The Online Encyclopedia of Integer Sequences (OEIS) catalog contains this sequence, which includes the numbers 1, 24, 1,560, and 119,580.

Have you heard of Belphegor's prime? This number is 1, which is followed by 13 zeros, then 666, followed by another 13 zeros, and finally, 1.

Cryptic Codes, Ciphers, and the Secrets of Cryptography

Cryptic codes, ciphers, and cryptography are all related to the practice of secure communication and information protection.

- **Cryptic codes:** These are systems of symbols or words used to convey hidden messages. Codes can replace words or phrases with other words, symbols, or numbers, making the original message indecipherable without knowledge of the code system.
- **Ciphers:** A cipher is a specific technique for transforming a message to keep it secret. There are different types of ciphers, including substitution ciphers (where letters are replaced by other letters) and transposition ciphers (where the order of letters is rearranged).
- **Cryptography:** This is the broader field that encompasses both cryptic codes and ciphers. Cryptography involves creating written or generated codes that allow information to be kept secure and is used in various applications,

from securing communications to protecting data in cybersecurity.

→ Together, these elements play a crucial role in ensuring privacy and security in communications, especially in the digital age.

Here are some interesting facts about cryptic codes, ciphers, and cryptography:

→ Cryptography dates back to ancient civilizations, including the Egyptians and Greeks, who used simple substitutions to hide messages.

→ The term "cryptography" comes from the Greek words *kryptos*, meaning "hidden," and *grapho*, meaning "to write."

→ The Caesar cipher, named after Julius Caesar, is one of the oldest known ciphers and shifts letters by a fixed number in the alphabet.

→ Morse code is a method that translates the letters and numbers into signals. It was named after Samuel Morse, one of the early developers of the system used for electrical telegraphy.

→ SOS is the international signal used to show extreme distress, especially by ships at sea.

→ The Enigma machine used by the Germans during World War II was a complex electromechanical device for encrypting messages.

→ Alan Turing, a mathematician and logician, played a crucial role in breaking the Enigma code, which significantly aided the Allied war effort.

→ The one-time pad cipher is considered the only theoretically unbreakable cipher when used correctly, as it uses a random key as long as the message itself.

→ The Playfair cipher, invented by Charles Wheatstone, encrypts pairs of letters to make them harder to break.

→ Modern cryptography relies heavily on mathematics, particularly on problems like prime factorization and discrete logarithms for security.

→ Public key cryptography, developed in the 1970s, allows secure communication using two keys: a public key for encryption and a private key for decryption.

→ The RSA algorithm, named after its inventors Rivest, Shamir, and Adleman, is one of the first public key cryptosystems.

→ Secure Sockets Layer (SSL) certificates use cryptographic protocols to secure data sent over the internet.

→ Hash functions create a fixed-size hash value from input data, making it easy to verify data integrity without revealing the original data.

→ The concept of a digital signature uses cryptography to provide authenticity and non-repudiation for digital messages or documents.

→ The Vigenère cipher is a method of encrypting alphabetic text using a simple form of polyalphabetic substitution.

→ Steganography is the practice of hiding a message within another message or medium, often used alongside cryptography.

→ Cryptanalysis is the field focused on breaking codes and ciphers, seeking vulnerabilities in cryptographic systems.

→ The phrase "the key to security is secrecy" refers to the

importance of keeping cryptographic keys safe to maintain security.

→ Cryptography plays a crucial role in securing communications in various fields, including finance, government, and personal privacy. So if you have an interest in this area, maybe think about these careers when you grow up!

→ As technology evolves, so do cryptographic methods, with quantum cryptography currently being researched for its potential to increase public security.

Surprising Facts

The term "cipher" originally referred to a method of writing that involved using a number to represent each letter, derived from the Arabic word *sifr,* which means "zero" or "empty." This reflects the early connection between numerals and secret writing.

Did you know that the oldest attempt at encryption dates back to Ancient Egypt? It's true! The oldest known encryption was found on the tomb of Khnumhotep II in Egypt around 2000 B.C.E. However, some believe that it might be a joke or an attempt to make his final resting place more mystical and mysterious.

Mathematical Riddle

I am a three-digit number. My tens digit is five more than my ones digit. My hundreds digit is eight less than my tens digit. What number am I?

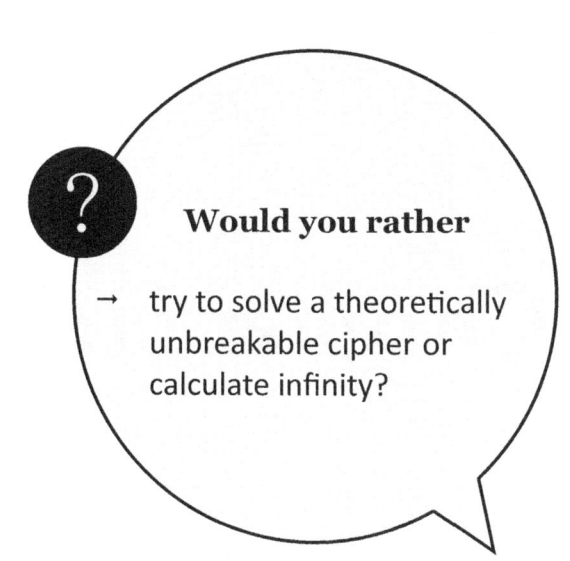

> **Would you rather**
> → try to solve a theoretically unbreakable cipher or calculate infinity?

Quiz

- ☐ What is the name of the world's oldest known cipher and who was it named after?
- ☐ What number is the golden ratio approximately equal to?
- ☐ What number is special because it has the same number of letters as the number itself?
- ☐ In which type of sequence is each number the sum of the two previous numbers, starting with 0 and 1?
- ☐ What do we call a number that reads the same forward and backward, like 121?
- ☐ Who played a key role in breaking the Enigma code during World War II?
- ☐ What does SOS stand for, and where is it commonly used?

Chapter Eight

Scrumptious Science of Food

---△---

Food is an essential part of our lives, but there's so much more to it than just satisfying our hunger. This chapter takes you on a delicious journey into the scrumptious science behind some of your favorite foods. From the tiny organisms that make bread rise to the antioxidants that turn berries into superfoods, you'll discover how chemistry and biology play a big role in what ends up on your plate.

Yummy Revelations About Your Favorite Foods

Food is more than just sustenance; it's an experience that connects us to culture, emotion, and creativity. From the tantalizing aroma of spices wafting through the air to the visual feast of vibrant, colorful dishes, food captivates our senses and brings people together. The joy of sharing a meal, exploring new flavors, and savoring each bite creates memories that linger long after the last crumb is gone. Whether it's comfort food that warms the heart or gourmet creations that dazzle the palate, the appeal of food lies in its ability to nourish not just the body but also the soul.

Here are some interesting facts about all of your favorite foods:

Bread

- Bread is one of the oldest prepared foods, dating back to at least 14,000 years ago.
- There are over 200 types of bread worldwide.
- Sourdough is one of the earliest forms of leavened bread (bread containing a rising agent, such as yeast, that causes the dough to rise).
- Gluten, a protein found in wheat, gives bread its chewy texture.
- The most popular bread in the world is white bread.

Fruit

- Bananas are berries, while strawberries are not. Strawberries are also the only fruit to have their seed on the outside.
- An apple floats in water because it is made of 25% air.
- Mangoes are known as the "king of fruits" in many cultures.
- Pineapples take about two years to grow before they can be harvested. Did you know they grow in the ground?
- Avocados are technically a fruit, and they grow on trees.

Vegetables

- Vegetables are full of vitamins and minerals. You need plenty of these in your diet to remain healthy!
- Carrots used to be purple but when orange ones began to appear, they became more popular, and the traditional purple carrots were replaced by the orange ones we know (and love) today.
- All vegetables are good for you, but different colored vegetables often have different nutrients. For example, orange vegetables are rich in beta-carotene, while the green ones are high in iron.
- A single red bell pepper contains more than 200% of the recommended daily dose of vitamin C.
- Peas are not always green. They come in several different varieties, including purple and yellow peas!

Savory Food

- The word "savory" comes from the Latin *sapor*, meaning "taste."
- Umami, the fifth taste, is often found in savory foods like tomatoes and mushrooms.
- Pizza originated in Naples, Italy, in the 18th century.
- The world's largest pizza was made in Rome and measured over 13,573 square feet.
- Did you know that saffron is the most expensive spice in the world? High-quality saffron can cost up to $5,000 per pound!

Chocolate

- → Chocolate is made from cacao beans, which grow on cacao trees. Cacao pods are similar in size to a pineapple and have about 40 cacao beans inside.
- → The first use of chocolate was by the Olmecs around 1000 B.C.E.
- → White chocolate, despite its name, contains no cocoa solids and is technically not chocolate.
- → The ancient Aztecs valued cacao beans so highly that they used them as a form of money. A turkey could be purchased for 100 cacao beans!
- → In Switzerland, people consume an average of 24 pounds of chocolate per person each year.

Surprising Facts

Honey never spoils. Archaeologists have found pots of honey in ancient Egyptian tombs that are over 3,000 years old and still perfectly edible.

A can of Diet Coke floats in water, but regular Coke sinks. It is believed that the sugar in regular Coke gives it the density to sink, while Diet Coke floats because it lacks sugar.

Peculiar Delicacies and Bizarre Cuisines

Exploring the world's unique and unusual foods is a journey through history, culture, and innovation. These cuisines offer fascinating insights into human creativity and survival. From ancient fermentation techniques to space-age meals, let's dive into the stories behind some of these extraordinary edibles.

Here are some curious facts about unusual foods and cuisines from around the world. These unusual foods highlight the diverse culinary traditions present in different cultures!

- Durian is known as the "king of fruits" in Southeast Asia, infamous for its strong odor that some find repulsive. It smells so bad that it is not allowed on public transport.
- Hákarl, a traditional Icelandic dish, is a fermented shark that is hung to dry for several months and has a very strong ammonia smell.
- Escamoles are edible ant larvae in Mexico, often referred to as "insect caviar" due to their taste and texture.
- In Japan, you can find odori ebi, a dish that features live shrimp served with soy sauce, which continues to move on the plate.
- Casu marzu, a traditional Sardinian cheese, is known for containing live insect larvae, which are intentionally introduced to aid fermentation.
- Century eggs, popular in China, are eggs cooked and preserved in a mix of clay, ash, and quicklime, giving them a unique flavor and dark color.

- Frog legs are a delicacy in France and some parts of the United States, such as South Carolina, Georgia, Florida, Mississippi, Alabama, and Louisiana, known for their mild flavor similar to chicken.
- Chapulines are a Mexican delicacy of toasted grasshoppers seasoned with lime juice, chili, and salt.
- Sannakji is a Korean dish made from a live octopus that is cut into small pieces and served immediately, still squirming on the plate.
- Paneer tikka, from India, features homemade cheese marinated in spices and grilled, often served skewered at festivals.
- Rocky Mountain oysters are not oysters at all, but deep-fried bull testicles, a novelty dish in certain Western U.S. states.
- In Sweden, surströmming is fermented herring that has such an overpowering smell that it's banned on public transport.
- Kiviak is an Inuit dish from Greenland where birds are fermented inside a seal's body and buried for several months before consumption.
- Insects like crickets and mealworms are becoming increasingly popular as food. Tempted?
- In Egypt, the tongues of sheep and cows (Lesan) are seasoned and cooked in boiling water.
- Rambutan is a fruit that surprises those who eat it because of its jelly-like texture!
- Black pudding, a type of blood sausage, is popular in the United Kingdom and made from pigs' blood and oatmeal.

- In Madagascar, zebu (a type of cattle) is often eaten grilled and is highly prized for its meat and milk.
- Deep-fried butter is a novelty item found at fairs in the United States, often served on a stick and covered in powdered sugar.
- Escargot, or cooked land snails, is a French delicacy typically prepared with garlic, butter, and parsley.
- In the Mediterranean, octopus salad is a popular dish often served with olive oil, lemon, and herbs.
- Nattō, a Japanese dish made from fermented soybeans, has a distinct smell and sticky texture, often served for breakfast.
- Poutine, originating from Quebec, is made of French fries topped with cheese curds and gravy, surprisingly delicious for its simplicity.
- In Bhutan, ema datshi is a spicy cheese and chili dish considered the country's national dish, highlighting local ingredients and flavors.
- Kangaroo meat in Australia is lean and high in protein, often grilled or made into sausages, capturing a unique taste of the land.

> **Surprising Facts**
>
> Kimchi, a staple in Korean cuisine, consists mainly of fermented cabbage with a mix of chili pepper, garlic, ginger, and fish sauce. Its origins date back over a thousand years, initially as a way to preserve vegetables during the harsh winter months. The preparation involves salting the cabbage to draw out moisture, mixing it with spices, and then allowing it to ferment for days or even months. This process not only enhances its flavor but also boosts its nutritional value by increasing beneficial bacteria that aid digestion and improve gut health.
>
> Space food innovations are a remarkable area of culinary science. Designed for astronauts on long missions, these foods must be nutritious, easy to store, and convenient to consume in zero gravity. Early space missions used basic items like freeze-dried powders and bite-sized cubes. However, modern technology has advanced to provide a wider array of options, including thermostabilized pouches and dehydrated meals that just need water.

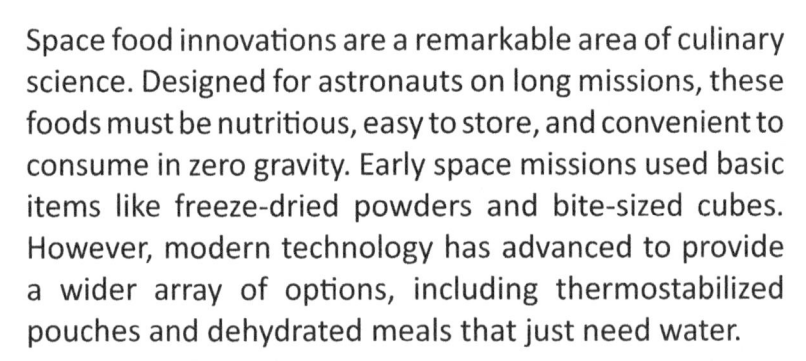

Extreme Eating Challenges and Outrageous Food Records

Let's dive into the fascinating and sometimes wild world of extreme eating and extraordinary food achievements! Competitive eating isn't just about gobbling up food; it's a blend of science, strategy, and sheer willpower. This section will explore how contestants train their bodies for these epic feasts, highlight some record-breaking foods, and touch upon the effects and ethical considerations of such practices.

Here are a few facts about eating challenges and food records:

- Eating challenges often arise from competitive eating events, where participants attempt to consume large quantities of food in a limited time.
- The famous Nathan's Hot Dog Eating Contest is held every Fourth of July in Coney Island, New York.
- Competitive eaters are often trained to expand their stomachs and consume foods in unique ways to maximize their intake.
- The current record for the most hot dogs eaten in 10 minutes is 76, set by Joey Chestnut in 2021.
- Eating challenges can have health risks, including potential choking hazards and digestive issues.
- Some restaurants create eating challenges to attract customers, often offering free meals or prizes for successful participants.
- Food records are often documented by organizations like the Guinness World Records, which verifies and tracks official records.
- The Big Texan Steak Ranch in Amarillo, Texas, features a 72-ounce steak challenge that must be eaten within 1 hour.
- Some challenges involve eating extremely spicy foods, like the "One Chip Challenge," which includes a single extremely spicy chip.
- Mukbang, a streaming trend originating in South Korea, involves hosts eating large quantities of food while engaging with their audience.

- Competitive eating is regulated by organizations, with specific rules and guidelines to ensure fair competition.
- The world record for most pancakes eaten in one sitting is 113, achieved by a competitive eater named Matt Stonie.
- Some challenges require participants to eat unusual combinations of food, testing their culinary limits and creativity.
- The "12 Egg Challenge" involves consuming a dozen raw eggs as quickly as possible, which can pose significant health risks.
- Some competitive eaters have unique techniques, such as "food dunking," where they soak food items in liquid to make swallowing easier.
- The famous dessert challenge at the *Diners, Drive-Ins and Dives* restaurants often features enormous sundaes or cake creations.
- Eating challenges can create viral content on social media platforms, leading to trends and a new generation of food influencers.
- In Japan, the "Giga Burger" challenge involves a massive burger weighing over 2.2 pounds, which must be completed in under 30 minutes.
- Some eating challenges are themed around pop culture, such as the "Lord of the Wings" challenge featuring a giant platter of chicken wings.
- The world record for the fastest time to eat a bowl of pasta is under 30 seconds.
- Some people participate in eating challenges for charitable causes, raising money through sponsorships for each food item consumed.

→ Many competitive eaters train by gradually increasing their food intake to build endurance and readiness for competitions.

→ The concept of "food waste" is frequently discussed in the context of eating challenges, with concerns over the amount of discarded food. According to the U.S. Food and Drug Administration (FDA), 30–40% of food in the United States is wasted.

→ The world's largest ice cream sundae was created in 1988 in Edmonton, Canada, weighing over 52,911 pounds.

Surprising Facts

You'd think that gobbling down dozens of hot dogs would be purely about having a massive appetite, but there's actually a lot more to it. For competitive eaters, mastering the sport means rigorous training. They start by stretching their stomachs to accommodate more food. This might sound odd, but they drink gallons of water or consume large amounts of low-calorie foods like vegetables to expand their stomach capacity (Parkhurst Ferguson, 2014).

Training for competitive eating competitions includes learning to control the gag reflex and practicing techniques to swallow faster. Speed is crucial in competitions, so many eaters practice by timing themselves while consuming various food types. Each type of food requires different techniques—for example, dipping buns in water to make them easier to swallow during hot dog contests.

Funky Flavors and Surprising Taste Sensations

Funky flavors often refer to unique, unconventional tastes that can surprise and delight the palate. They can include anything from savory combinations like miso and caramel to sweet surprises such as lavender-infused desserts. Ingredients such as kumquats, exotic spices, and herbs can elevate traditional dishes, creating unexpected flavor profiles. Each flavor can evoke different emotions and memories, making the dining experience more memorable. Surprising taste sensations might also come from contrasts, like sweet and sour or spicy and creamy, which can create a dynamic balance that excites the taste buds. Culinary experimentation continues to push boundaries, inviting food enthusiasts to explore a world of tastes that challenge their expectations.

Here are some flavorful facts about funky flavors and surprising taste sensations:

- → Sriracha sauce combines sweet, spicy, and tangy flavors, making it a versatile condiment.
- → The sweetness of ripe fruit can be enhanced by unconventional spices like cayenne pepper.
- → Foie gras, a delicacy made from duck or goose liver, has a rich, buttery flavor that many find surprising.
- → Lavender can be used in both sweet and savory dishes, adding a floral note that's unexpectedly delightful.
- → The flavor of matcha, a powdered green tea, is earthy and slightly sweet, with a creamy mouthfeel.
- → Pickling vegetables can create tangy flavors that transform ordinary produce into something extraordinary.

- Dragon fruit has a mildly sweet flavor and a striking appearance, often surprising those who try it.
- Sweet and savory combinations like bacon and chocolate are trending for their surprising contrasts.
- Celery root or celeriac offers a nutty, earthy flavor that can be unexpected in mashed forms.
- The umami taste can be amplified using ingredients like miso, soy sauce, and seaweed.
- The spice fenugreek has a sweet, nutty flavor reminiscent of maple, often used in Indian cuisine.
- Yuzu is a Japanese citrus fruit offering a tart and fragrant flavor that excites the palate.
- The texture of boba (tapioca pearls) combined with sweetened milk tea creates a unique sensation.
- Smoked ingredients, such as smoked salt or smoked paprika, can add depth and complexity to dishes.
- Chocolate-covered insects are a delicacy in some cultures, combining rich chocolate with crunchy protein.
- Fermented foods like kimchi and sauerkraut have a tangy flavor and health benefits due to probiotics.
- The flavor of rosemary can enhance meats and bread, adding a woodsy note that's unexpected yet pleasing.
- Candied jalapeños offer a surprising balance of heat and sweetness for toppings or snacks.
- Coconut water has a mildly sweet, nutty flavor and is a hydrating drink with unexpected versatility.
- Sweet potatoes can provide a sweet and earthy flavor that surprises those who expect only savory.

→ The combination of sweet and salty, like salted caramel, creates a complex flavor experience that's addictive.

Surprising Facts

The perceptions of taste are subjective and can change based on context. For example, studies have shown that people tend to perceive sweet foods as more pleasant when they are in a happy or relaxed mood, while the same food may be viewed less favorably in stressful situations (Mastinu et al., 2023).

There are ice cream flavors like garlic, wasabi, and even avocado, showcasing the unique and often surprising combinations that can appeal to adventurous taste buds!

Would you rather

→ consume kangaroo meat or Rocky Mountain oysters?

→ participate in a 72-ounce steak challenge in 1 hour or 113 pancakes in a single sitting?

→ eat a chocolate-covered insect or complete the "12 Egg Challenge"?

Quiz

- ☐ How many pounds of chocolate does the average Swiss citizen eat each year?
- ☐ How many hot dogs did Joey Chestnut eat in 10 minutes in 2021?
- ☐ Why do apples float in water?
- ☐ Which vegetable used to be purple before the orange version became popular?
- ☐ What fruit is called the "king of fruits" in Southeast Asia and is banned on public transport because of its strong smell?
- ☐ What traditional Sardinian cheese contains live insect larvae to help with fermentation?
- ☐ Which Chinese delicacy is made from eggs preserved in a mix of clay, ash, and quicklime?
- ☐ What organization often documents official food records, like eating challenges?
- ☐ What unexpected spice can enhance the sweetness of ripe fruit?

Chapter Nine

Mysteries of History

---△---

Understanding the past is like piecing together a giant puzzle with many missing pieces. History is filled with fascinating mysteries that capture our imagination and make us wonder about the lives of those who came before us. From ancient ruins to puzzling artifacts, these mysteries challenge us to look deeper into what we think we know. Have you ever wondered why some great civilizations vanished or how people built incredible structures without modern technology?

In this chapter, we're diving into the enigmas of lost civilizations. Get ready to travel back in time and unravel the secrets of these ancient worlds.

Lost Civilizations

The mysteries of ancient civilizations have fascinated historians and archaeologists for centuries. These enigmatic cultures leave behind only fragments of their existence, prompting us to piece together their stories and understand their sudden disappearances. In exploring lost civilizations, we gain valuable insights into human resilience, adaptation, and innovation.

Here are some facts about lost ancient civilizations:

→ The Indus Valley Civilization, located in present-day Pakistan and northwest India, was one of the world's earliest urban cultures, thriving around 2500 B.C.E. At that time, 10% of the world's population lived in the Indus Valley and used toilet seats made from brick.

→ The Maya civilization, known for its advanced writing system and calendar, reached its peak around 250–900 C.E. in present-day Mexico, Belize, Guatemala, and Honduras. It was the Mayans who invented chocolate!

→ Ancient Greece is remembered today for its lively collection of gods and goddesses and the stories they told about them. Did you know that the Ancient Greeks used pebbles as toilet paper? Ouch!

→ The Olmec civilization, often considered the "mother culture" of Mesoamerica, flourished around 1200–400 B.C.E. and is known for its large stone heads.

→ The Sumerians, who inhabited ancient Mesopotamia (modern-day Iraq), are credited with inventing one of the first writing systems, cuneiform, around 3200 B.C.E.

→ The city of Petra, once the thriving capital of the Nabataean Kingdom, was an essential trading hub in ancient times, known for its stunning rock-cut architecture and water conduit system.

→ The Harappan civilization is noted for its advanced drainage systems, which showcase sophisticated engineering.

→ Teotihuacan in ancient Mexico was known for its massive pyramids, including the Pyramid of the Sun and the Pyramid of the Moon.

- The Ancestral Puebloans, also known as the Anasazi, built cliff dwellings in the American Southwest, with notable sites like Mesa Verde and Chaco Canyon.
- The Khmer Empire in Southeast Asia, particularly known for the magnificent temple complex of Angkor Wat, thrived from the 9th to the 15th centuries.
- The Etruscans, who inhabited parts of ancient Italy before the rise of Rome, invented focaccia bread!
- The Chavín civilization in Peru is known for its religious and artistic achievements, flourishing between 900 and 200 B.C.E. They were feminists as all the highest priests were women.
- The city of Cahokia, located near modern-day St. Louis, was once North America's largest urban settlement, flourishing from 600 to 1400 C.E. with cool earthen mounds.
- The Byzantine Empire, a continuation of the Roman Empire in the east, fell to the Ottoman Turks in 1453. Its capital city, Byzantium, was famous for its entertainments such as chariot races, plays, and the annual carnival, Apokreas.
- The civilization of Great Zimbabwe was known for its stunning stone ruins and as a center of trade in southeastern Africa between the 11th and 15th centuries.
- The Nazca culture in ancient Peru is famous for the Nazca Lines—massive geoglyphs with large-scale patterns etched into the desert floor by humans using rocks and soil or removing ground cover. Their purpose remains a mystery to this day.

> **Surprising Facts**
>
> You probably haven't heard of them, but the Caral–Supe civilization from the Supe Valley of Peru was the earliest known civilization to exist in the American continents nearly 4,600 years ago.
>
> Many ancient civilizations, such as the Maya and the Romans, used a form of dental hygiene that included the use of chew sticks or even primitive forms of toothpaste made from natural ingredients like charcoal, ash, and tree bark. This shows that the importance of dental care has been recognized for thousands of years!

Legendary Treasures and Riches

The allure of legendary treasures has fascinated adventurers for generations. The stories of hidden riches and lost cities captivate imaginations and inspire endless quests even though no one knows if they really exist or not. Today, we'll journey through some of the most famous legendary treasures: El Dorado, the Knights Templar's hidden riches, King Solomon's mines, and Captain Kidd's pirate hoards.

These tales offer a thrilling entry point into history. They encourage curiosity about the past and a sense of wonder about the world's hidden secrets. And who knows? Perhaps one day, with enough determination and luck, one of you might be the one to finally uncover one of these long-lost treasures.

Here are some intriguing facts about legendary treasures and riches. These treasures, steeped in history and myth, continue to captivate adventurers and historians alike!

- The lost city of Atlantis located under the sea is often associated with great riches and advanced technology, captivating imaginations for centuries. No one knows if Atlantis really existed, but scientists are still searching! Plato, a famous philosopher, first wrote about it 2,500 years ago.

- The legend of El Dorado refers to a mythical city of gold in South America, drawing many explorers in search of wealth.

- The treasure of the Flor de la Mar, a sunken Portuguese ship, was lost in 1511. People still want to find it as it is believed to have carried a fortune worth millions.

- King Solomon's mines, mentioned in the Bible, are fabled to be filled with gold and precious stones, inspiring many treasure hunts.

- The Lost Mine of Ophir, a place of untold wealth mentioned in biblical texts, remains undiscovered and the subject of numerous theories.

- The Spanish galleons that sank during the 17th and 18th centuries, such as the Atocha, were often laden with gold and silver from the Americas.

- The Seven Cities of Gold (Cibola) were sought by Spanish conquistadors but were never found, fueling the legend of untold wealth in North America.

- The Black Pearl, reputedly owned by pirate Captain Jack Sparrow, symbolizes the allure of legendary treasures among pirate tales.

- The treasure of Oak Island, a site in Nova Scotia, Canada, has been the focus of treasure hunters for over 200 years, with various theories of hidden gold.
- The Crown Jewels of England are some of the most famous treasures, with a rich history including gold, diamonds, and other gemstones. They have been stored at the Tower of London since the 1660s.
- The SS Central America, a shipwreck from 1857, carried a fortune in gold and has inspired efforts to salvage its lost treasure.
- The legendary treasure of the hidden copper scrolls, linked to Chinese miners in the 19th century, is believed to be hidden in the Sierra Nevada mountains.
- The story of the Beechworth gold, supposedly hidden in Australia, is a local legend that attracts treasure hunters.
- The treasure hidden by notorious outlaw Jesse James is rumored to be buried in various locations across the American West.
- The Lost Dutchman's Gold Mine is a fabled gold mine in Arizona that has never been found, despite many searches.
- In 2014, a treasure hunter discovered a hoard of artifacts and gold coins in the Schatzalp area of Switzerland, worth millions.
- The legend of the Knights Templar and their lost treasure, believed to be hidden after the Templar's demise, continues to inspire searches and tales.

> **Surprising Facts**
>
> The treasure of the Spanish galleon Nuestra Señora de Atocha, which sank off the Florida Keys in 1622, was estimated to be worth over $400 million when it was discovered in 1985, making it one of the richest shipwrecks ever found.
>
> The tomb of Tutankhamun, discovered in 1922 by Howard Carter, contained over 5,000 artifacts, including a golden funerary mask and intricate jewelry, leading to a frenzy of fascination and study about ancient Egyptian burial practices and wealth beyond what was expected for a pharaoh of his age.

Secrets of Iconic Monuments and Amazing Ancient Architecture

The idea of uncovering hidden truths behind iconic monuments and architectural marvels is fascinating. Iconic monuments and ancient architecture are some of the most impressive human creations, reflecting the values, technologies, and artistic sensibilities of their respective eras. Such monuments and architectural styles tell stories of their civilizations, embodying cultural significance, artistry, and historical importance.

Here are some facts about iconic monuments and ancient architecture:

- → The Great Pyramid of Giza is 48 feet tall and weighs 5.7 million tons. It is the oldest of the Seven Wonders of the Ancient World and is the only one to remain largely intact.

- Machu Picchu, an Inca fortress, was built in the 15th century by the Inca Empire and is located in the Andes Mountains of Peru.
- The Colosseum in Rome could hold up to 80,000 spectators and was used for gladiatorial contests and public spectacles.
- The Parthenon in Athens, which is 45 feet at its highest point, was dedicated to the ancient Greek goddess Athena.
- Angkor Wat in Cambodia is the largest religious monument in the world and originally served as a Hindu temple before becoming a Buddhist site.
- The Taj Mahal in India was built by Mughal Emperor Shah Jahan in memory of his wife Mumtaz Mahal and is a symbol of love. It took about 22 years to build with about 20,000 workers. Construction was completed in 1647.
- Stonehenge in England is a prehistoric monument that dates back to around 3000 B.C.E. and is believed to have been used for ceremonial purposes.
- The Eiffel Tower in Paris was completed in 1889 for the Exposition Universelle and stands at 1,083 feet tall.
- The Acropolis of Athens is a UNESCO World Heritage site and includes several ancient buildings of great architectural and historic significance. Acropolis means "high city."
- The Great Wall of China stretches over 13,000 miles and was constructed to protect against invasions and raids.
- The Sagrada Família in Barcelona has never been completed although it has been under construction since 1882!
- The moai of Easter Island are monolithic statues that were carved by the Rapa Nui people and are a symbol of their culture. There are over 880 statues, the biggest is Paro, which is 30 feet tall and weighs 90 tons!

- Chichen Itza in Mexico was a major Mayan city known for its iconic pyramid, El Castillo, which is a UNESCO World Heritage Site.
- The Roman Pantheon, completed around 126 A.D., is known for its large dome and oculus, which is still the world's largest unreinforced concrete dome.
- Neuschwanstein Castle in Germany was commissioned by Ludwig II and is often cited as an inspiration for Disney's *Sleeping Beauty* castle.

Surprising Facts

The intricate design of Machu Picchu also holds spiritual meaning, as it was likely built to honor Inti, the sun god. Each stone was expertly cut to fit together so precisely that even a knife blade couldn't fit between them. This level of precision reveals not only the Incas's technical prowess but also their deep connection to the natural world and their deities.

Stonehenge stands on Salisbury Plain in England and continues to baffle historians and archaeologists alike. Erected during the late Neolithic period, this stone circle consists of enormous sarsen stones and smaller bluestones transported from Pembrokeshire. Evidence suggests part of the stone circle was initially built near the Pembrokeshire coast before being dismantled and reconstructed 176 miles down the road in Wiltshire!

Mysterious Disappearances of People, Places, and Things

Mysterious disappearances have long captivated human imagination, spanning a variety of subjects from people to places and objects. Here are a few intriguing examples in each category. These examples highlight humanity's fascination with the unknown, prompting investigations, theories, and captivating stories.

Here are some facts about missing people, places, and things:

- The USS Pickering was caught up in a hurricane that swept Florida and the Bahamas on September 20, 1800, and has never been found since.
- The case of Malaysia Airlines Flight 370, which disappeared in 2014, remains one of the greatest aviation mysteries.
- More than 600,000 individuals are reported missing in the United States each year.
- The USS Cyclops disappeared between the Bahamas and Baltimore, Maryland, between March 4 and 13, 1918. No contact was made from the ship despite it having a wireless radio onboard. No trace of her has ever been found.
- The Bermuda Triangle is infamous for the mysterious disappearances of ships and aircraft over its waters.
- The case of the Sodder children, who vanished from their home in 1945 after a fire, remains unsolved to this day.
- In ancient history, explorers often went missing in uncharted territories, leading to legends about lost civilizations, such as the underwater civilization of Atlantis.

- The merchant ship, Mary Celeste, was deserted by her crew in the Atlantic Ocean off the Azores islands on December 4, 1872. They have never been seen since.
- Amelia Earhart, the famous aviator, disappeared in 1937 during a flight around the world and her fate is still uncertain.
- The Ourang Medan is a legendary ghost ship that reportedly was found in Indonesian waters in the 1940s. Distress signals claimed that the crew had perished, with inexplicable circumstances surrounding their deaths. When rescuers boarded the ship, they found the crew dead with horrified expressions on their faces. The ship itself was said to have been abandoned and mysteriously sank shortly thereafter.
- The DNA Doe Project works to discover unidentified remains and connect them with missing persons' cases using genetic genealogy.
- MV Joyita was a merchant vessel that vanished in 1955 while sailing from Samoa to Tokelau. When it was eventually found adrift a month later, the ship was in disarray, and all but one of the crew members were missing. Why they disappeared remains a mystery.
- Some iconic places, like Atlantis, are said to be lost to time and are often referenced as "missing" parts of history.

> **Surprising Facts**
>
> In 1587, a group of English settlers established a colony on Roanoke Island, only to vanish without a trace. When a supply ship returned three years later, the only clue left was the word "Croatoan" carved into a tree.
>
> Flight 19 is one of the most famous incidents associated with the Bermuda Triangle. On December 5, 1945, five Avenger torpedo bombers from the U.S. Navy, collectively known as Flight 19, went missing during a training flight over the Atlantic Ocean. The planes encountered navigation difficulties, and despite the dispatch of a rescue plane, that aircraft also disappeared. No trace of the planes or their crews was ever found, leading to various theories and speculations about their fate.

Cracking the Codes of Ancient Writings and Dead Languages

Ancient writings refer to the earliest forms of written communication that emerged in various cultures around the world, often using different scripts and languages. Meanwhile, dead languages are languages that no longer have native speakers or are no longer spoken conversationally. Ancient writings and dead languages contribute significantly to our understanding of history, culture, and the development of human communication.

Here are some interesting facts about ancient writings and dead languages:

- → The oldest known writing system is cuneiform, developed by the Sumerians around 3200 B.C.E. in ancient Mesopotamia.

- Egyptian hieroglyphs (an alphabet where pictures represent objects and letters) date back to around 3100 B.C.E. and were used for over 3,000 years.
- The Indus Valley Civilization developed a script around 2600 B.C.E., which remains undeciphered to this day.
- The Rosetta Stone, discovered in 1799, was crucial for deciphering Egyptian hieroglyphs as it contained the same text in Greek, demotic, and hieroglyphic script.
- Linear B, an early form of Greek, was used by the Mycenaeans from around 1450 to 1200 B.C.E. and was deciphered in the 1950s.
- The Phoenician alphabet, developed around 1200 B.C.E., is considered one of the ancestors of modern alphabets, including Greek and Latin.
- Aramaic was a widespread lingua franca (a common language between speakers whose native languages are different) in the Near East and the language of significant biblical texts, including portions of the Old Testament.
- Sanskrit, an ancient Indian language, has a rich literary heritage and is the religious language of Hinduism.
- Ancient Chinese script, known as oracle bone script, dates back to the Shang Dynasty around 1200 B.C.E. and evolved into modern Chinese characters.
- The Etruscan language, spoken by the Etruscans in ancient Italy, is largely undeciphered and remains a mystery to linguists.
- The Mayan script, used by the ancient Mayans, is one of the few fully developed writing systems in pre-Columbian America.

→ The Ugaritic script, discovered in modern-day Syria, dates back to around 1400 B.C.E. and provides insight into ancient Near Eastern cultures.

→ Latin, originally spoken by the Romans, became the dominant language of the Roman Empire and evolved into the Romance languages.

→ The Pictish language, spoken by the Picts in ancient Scotland, is known from symbols and inscriptions, but we don't know where it came from.

→ The Vendidad, part of the Avesta collection of religious literature of the Zoroastrian religion, containing some of its oldest texts, was written in Avestan, an ancient Iranian language.

→ The Gnostic texts, written in Coptic or Greek, are significant for understanding early Christian and Gnostic beliefs.

→ The Olmec civilization had a proto-writing system that is one of the earliest known in Mesoamerica, although details about it are scarce.

Surprising Facts

Some examples of ancient forms of writing are the following:

- **Cuneiform:** Developed by the Sumerians around 3400 B.C.E., this script was inscribed on clay tablets and is considered one of the earliest systems of writing.
- **Hieroglyphics:** Used in ancient Egypt, hieroglyphics combined logographic and alphabetic elements. They were often carved into stone or written on papyrus.
- **Chinese characters:** The earliest known Chinese writing dates back to around 1200 B.C.E. and was inscribed on oracle bones. This system has evolved into the complex character set used today.
- **Phoenician alphabet:** This script, developed around 1050 B.C.E., is one of the earliest forms of alphabetic writing and is the ancestor of many modern alphabets.

Three examples of dead languages are as follows:

- **Latin:** Once the lingua franca of the Roman Empire, Latin is still used in specific contexts, such as in the Catholic Church or scientific nomenclature.
- **Sanskrit:** An ancient language of India, Sanskrit is used in Hindu scriptures and classical literature but is not spoken as a native language today.
- **Ancient Greek:** While Modern Greek is spoken today, Ancient Greek, the language of classical literature and philosophy, is considered a dead language.

Odd Obsessions of Famous Historical Figures

Many famous historical figures had peculiar obsessions that shaped their lives and, in some cases, their work. These obsessions often drove their creativity but also contributed to their struggles with mental health and relationships.

Here are some intriguing facts about the odd obsessions of historical figures. These odd obsessions offer a unique glimpse into their lives!

- → Emperor Napoleon Bonaparte of France was obsessed with the number 13 and had a particular aversion to it, believing it to bring bad luck.
- → King Charles II of England was fascinated with animal pets and kept various unusual animals, including a pet monkey and even a lion.
- → British Prime Minister Winston Churchill had a passion for painting and would often escape the pressures of politics by creating artwork.
- → Famous psychoanalyst Sigmund Freud collected ancient relics and was obsessed with antiquities, especially Egyptian artifacts.
- → Howard Hughes, the reclusive billionaire, was obsessed with cleanliness and would often refuse to touch things without wearing gloves.
- → Composer Ludwig van Beethoven had a peculiar habit of being overly particular about the temperature of his water and only drinking it at certain times.

- Artist Vincent van Gogh had a fixation on yellow and often painted with the color to the point where he believed it held a special significance.
- U.S. President Benjamin Franklin documented his daily habits obsessively, creating a rigorous schedule to improve his productivity.
- The actress and movie star Marilyn Monroe had a strange obsession with books and often read them obsessively, trying to enhance her intellect.
- Greek emperor Alexander the Great was famously obsessed with his horse, Bucephalus, even going so far as to share a strong sense of empathy with him.
- The Egyptian empress Cleopatra was fascinated by perfumes and cosmetics, dedicating a large part of her wealth to acquiring and crafting them.
- U.S. President Thomas Jefferson was a fervent collector of books and obsessed with creating one of the largest private libraries in America.
- Artist Pablo Picasso had an obsession with creating art at an astonishing pace, producing thousands of pieces and experimenting with styles.
- Mathematician Albert Einstein had a peculiar habit of playing the violin to help him think and solve complex problems.
- British Queen Victoria had a fascination with mourning jewelry and often commissioned pieces to remember deceased loved ones.
- U.S. President Richard Nixon was obsessed with politics to the extent that he even kept a scrapbook of his own press clippings.

→ Artist Frida Kahlo had a deep love for pets, especially her many dogs and monkeys, finding companionship in their presence.

Surprising Facts

Leonardo da Vinci: The legendary artist and inventor had a fixation with the number three. He often structured his paintings and projects in groups of three, believing it held a special significance. This can be seen in his painting *The Last Supper,* which contains several references to that number.

Nikola Tesla: Mathematician Tesla had a phobia of germs and a strong obsession with cleanliness. He would wash his hands frequently and avoided touching anything that he considered dirty, which at times hindered his social life.

Would you rather

→ crack the code of a lost ancient language or discover what happened to a missing person?

→ look after King Charles II's lion or one of Frida Kahlo's monkeys?

→ walk the length of the Great Wall of China or count all the spectators at the Colosseum in Rome when it was full?

Quiz

- ☐ Which ancient civilization used brick toilet seats around 2500 B.C.E.?
- ☐ Who invented chocolate?
- ☐ What is the name of the legendary underwater city full of riches and amazing technology that people are still searching for?
- ☐ What is the name of the fabled gold mine in Arizona that has never been found?
- ☐ Which ancient structure is the only one of the Seven Wonders of the Ancient World that remains largely intact?
- ☐ Which famous aviator disappeared during a flight around the world in 1937?
- ☐ What is the oldest known writing system, and who developed it?
- ☐ Which writing system was used by the ancient Egyptians for over 3,000 years?
- ☐ Which famous mathematician played the violin to help solve complex problems?
- ☐ What color was Vincent van Gogh obsessed with and often used in his paintings?

Chapter Ten

Odds and Ends

When it comes to strange and quirky facts, there are plenty of oddities that don't quite fit into any single category. These odds and ends may seem random at first glance, but they reveal fascinating insights into different cultures and histories. From bizarre laws still on the books to peculiar traditions and unusual phobias, this chapter dives into a variety of weird and wonderful topics that will leave you both entertained and curious.

In this chapter, you'll discover some of the most unexpected facts that didn't have a place elsewhere in the book. Get ready to be amazed by these odd bits of trivia that prove truth is often stranger than fiction!

Weird Laws Still on the Books Around the World

When it comes to bizarre laws, the world is full of them. Some countries still enforce outdated and peculiar regulations that seem almost too strange to be true. Have you ever wondered why it's illegal to let your chickens cross the road in Quitman, Georgia? Or why holding a salmon under suspicious circumstances in England could land you in trouble? These quirky laws might make you scratch your head, but they also shed light on the historical and cultural contexts from which they arose.

While these strange and unusual laws might seem laughable, each one carries its own historical and cultural significance. They demonstrate that legal systems worldwide are complex and often reflect the unique values and concerns of their societies. Understanding these laws helps us appreciate the diverse ways communities have evolved to manage issues pertinent to their times. Plus, knowing about these quirky regulations can certainly make for entertaining dinner table conversation!

Here are some facts about weird laws from various places around the world. These laws may sound odd, but they reflect different cultural values and legal interpretations!

- In Switzerland, it is illegal to own just one guinea pig because they are social animals and need companionship.
- In France, it is against the law to name a pig "Napoleon."
- In Singapore, it is illegal to chew gum, with exceptions for medicinal purposes.
- In Victoria, Australia, doing business with pirates is illegal and can result in a 10-year prison sentence.
- In Massachusetts, it is illegal to have a gorilla in the backseat of your car.
- In Italy, dying in the town of Falciano del Massico is prohibited; residents must leave the town to die.
- In Los Angeles, it's illegal for a waiter to bring you a side of lettuce with your meal if it's not requested.
- In Denmark, it is illegal to start a vehicle if there is a person underneath it.
- In Canada, it is illegal to remove a bandage in public.

- In Portugal, you can be fined for not having a shower before heading to the beach.
- In Scotland, it is legal to kill a Scottish deerhound if it is harassing you while you are carrying a bow and arrow.
- In Honolulu, it's illegal to place a coin in your ear.
- In Spain, you may be fined for wearing a bikini outside of a designated beach area.
- In Rome, eating on public transport can lead to a fine.
- In Ohio, it is against the law to get a fish drunk.
- In New York City, it's illegal to take more than three sips of beer while standing up.
- In Japan, it is illegal to dance after midnight in clubs.
- In Thailand, it is illegal to step on money, as it is considered disrespectful to the king.
- In Georgia, it's illegal to drive with a chicken in your lap.

> **Surprising Facts**
>
> Did you know that in England and Wales, it is illegal to hold salmon in suspicious circumstances? It's true! Section 32 of the Salmon Act 1986 says it is an offense for any person to receive or dispose of salmon in any circumstances where there is a reasonable suspicion that it could have been illegally fished.
>
> In Milan, Italy, it is a legal requirement to smile at all times. Except at funerals or in hospitals. This regulation was put in place at the time Milan was under the rule of the Austro-Hungarian Empire (1740–1859) and was never repealed.

Strange Competitions, Holidays, and Celebrations

Did you know that around the world, people gather to celebrate some of the quirkiest and most unusual festivals? These unique events provide a fascinating look at diverse cultures and bring communities together in surprising ways. These events bring people together in ways that go beyond ordinary social interactions. Whether through friendly competition, artistic endeavors, or downright silly activities, these events strengthen community bonds and showcase the unique characteristics of each culture. They remind us that even the most peculiar traditions can be meaningful and joyous.

Here are some interesting facts about weird competitions, holidays, and celebrations. These events certainly add a unique flair to the celebration calendar!

- → The World Beard and Moustache Championships celebrate facial hair with categories for different styles and lengths.
- → The annual Wife Carrying Championship in Finland has male competitors racing while carrying their wives over an obstacle course.
- → The National Hound Dog Trials in the United States pits dog owners against each other in a series of hunting challenges with their beagles.
- → The Cooper's Hill Cheese-Rolling and Wake in Gloucestershire, England, involves participants chasing a wheel of cheese down a steep hill.
- → In Japan, the Naki Sumo Crying Baby Festival features sumo wrestlers trying to make babies cry; the loudest baby wins!
- → The Great American Beard and Moustache Championship in Michigan celebrates hairstyles with contests for full beards, mustaches, and more.

- The Great Pacific Garbage Patch cleanup is a competition where teams race against the clock to collect trash from the ocean.
- The World Porridge Making Championship in Scotland invites chefs from around the world to showcase their porridge-cooking skills.
- The World Toe Wrestling Championship in Derbyshire, England, has competitors lock their toes and try to pin each other down.
- La Tomatina in Spain involves a massive tomato fight where thousands of people throw ripe tomatoes at each other.
- The Air Guitar World Championships in Finland allows participants to compete by performing air guitar routines on stage.
- The Running of the Bulls in Pamplona, Spain, sees daring participants run in front of a group of bulls through the city streets.
- The International Cherry Pit-Spitting Championship in Michigan tests competitors' distance spitting skills with cherry pits.
- The Idaho Potato Drop is an annual New Year's Eve celebration that features a giant potato being dropped from a crane at midnight.
- The World Elephant Polo Championship in Thailand features teams of players riding elephants to score goals in a traditional polo match.
- Global Smurf Day is celebrated on the first Saturday of September, encouraging people all over the world to dress up as Smurfs.

- The Chocolate Festival in London showcases chocolate-related dishes and hosts competitions for chocolate sculpting.
- The Mermaid Parade in Coney Island, New York, celebrates the beginning of summer with a colorful procession of mermaid-themed floats and costumes.
- The World Snail Racing Championship in Norfolk, United Kingdom, involves snails racing on a circular track, with the fastest player winning a prize.

> **Surprising Facts**
>
> La Tomatina, held in Buñol, Spain, is the world's biggest food fight. This festival sees thousands of people pelting each other with ripe tomatoes. Held on the last Wednesday of August, La Tomatina begins with a blast of water cannons, signaling the start of an hour-long tomato fight. The streets turn red, and everyone becomes covered in squishy, juicy tomatoes. While the origins of the festival are a bit murky, it's believed to have started in 1945, and its popularity has only grown since then. This annual event highlights the playful and spirited nature of the local community, drawing visitors from all over the world who want to join in the fun.
>
> Scarecrow Fest held in the United States is where townspeople create life-size scarecrows and display them throughout the town. These scarecrows range from traditional to humorous depictions of famous characters. Visitors stroll through the streets to admire the creativity on display, fostering a sense of pride and unity within the town. It's a light-hearted and imaginative way for the community to express themselves and engage with one another.

Puzzling Phobias and Fears

Imagine waking up one day and feeling an overwhelming sense of fear just by looking at a honeycomb, the inside of a pomegranate, or even a sponge. This is what life can be like for someone with trypophobia, an irrational fear of holes often clustered together in irregular patterns. People with this condition find themselves deeply uncomfortable or fearful at the sight of these objects, which might seem harmless to others.

Why should we care about these uncommon phobias? Delving into rare phobias like trypophobia can help us better understand how fear operates within the human mind and affects our mental health.

Here are a few facts about strange phobias and fears. Phobias can be unique and sometimes surprisingly specific!

- Arachibutyrophobia is the fear of peanut butter sticking to the roof of your mouth.
- Nomophobia is the fear of being without your mobile phone or losing signal.
- Xanthophobia is the fear of the color yellow.
- Triskaidekaphobia is the fear of the number 13.
- Ombrophobia is the fear of rain.
- Pteronophobia is the fear of being tickled by feathers.
- Anthophobia is the fear of flowers.
- Selenophobia is the fear of the moon.
- Chionophobia is the fear of snow.

- Phobophobia is the fear of developing a phobia.
- Cyberphobia is the fear of technology or the internet.
- Eisoptrophobia is the fear of mirrors or one's own reflection.
- Vestiphobia is the fear of clothing.
- Megalophobia is the fear of large objects.
- Coulrophobia is the fear of clowns.
- Ailurophobia is the fear of cats.
- Heliophobia is the fear of sunlight or the sun.
- Logophobia is the fear of words.
- Hippopotomonstrosesquippedaliophobia is ironically the fear of long words.

Surprising Facts

Did you know that mageirocophobia is the fear of cooking? Well, it's true. Perhaps some people just don't like to cook.

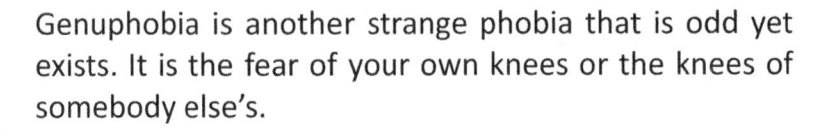

Genuphobia is another strange phobia that is odd yet exists. It is the fear of your own knees or the knees of somebody else's.

Crazy Coincidences and Astonishing Acts of Chance

Crazy coincidences and astonishing acts of chance often leave us amazed by the unpredictability of life. For instance, consider the famous story of two people who have the same dream on the same night or two strangers meeting in a foreign country only to discover they're long-lost relatives.

Sometimes, acts of chance can lead to incredible outcomes, like a misplaced letter ending up in the hands of the intended recipient years later due to a clerical error. These instances remind us how interconnected our lives can be and how randomness can create fascinating narratives that seem almost too incredible to be true!

Here are some intriguing facts about crazy coincidences and astonishing acts of chance:

- The "birthday paradox" states that in a group of just 23 people, there's a 50% chance that two people share the same birthday.
- In 1975, a man named William F. C. Pellett found himself seated next to a stranger on a flight who turned out to be his long-lost brother.
- In 2006, a woman named Rebecca Smith met another woman with the same name, same birthday, and same social security number.
- Two U.S. Presidents, Thomas Jefferson and John Adams died on the 50th anniversary of American independence (July 4, 1826).
- Abraham Lincoln and John F. Kennedy share several eerie coincidences. Both were assassinated on a Friday while

sitting next to their wives. Lincoln was shot in Ford's Theatre, and Kennedy was shot in a Lincoln car manufactured by Ford.

→ The likelihood of randomly selecting 2 people who have the same first name and last name is approximately 1 in 880,000.

→ In 1995, marathon runner Jim McElveen and actor Tom Hanks discovered they had the same birthday and were born in the same hospital.

→ A woman named Anne Sibert and her son, who lived on opposite coasts of the United States, both had the same car accident on the same day.

→ In 2007, a man named John McDonald was buried in a cemetery next to his son, who had died years earlier—both were named John McDonald.

→ In 1912, a man named John McGraw predicted the sinking of the Titanic based on a dream he had the night before.

→ The Titanic, which was famously "unsinkable" yet sank on its first voyage in 1912 and her sister ship, the Olympic, were almost identical. Interestingly, the Olympic had a series of accidents before the Titanic sank, including a collision with a warship. After the Titanic disaster, the Olympic was repaired and remained in service until 1935, while the Titanic's sinking created a lasting legacy.

→ When the tomb of Tutankhamun was discovered in 1922, several people involved in the excavation died under mysterious circumstances, leading to the belief in a "curse." However, many experts argue that it was due to infections or other causes, making the coincidence quite intriguing.

→ A woman found out that her best friend was her half sister after doing a DNA test. Half siblings share approximately 25% of their DNA.

→ The odds of a person winning the lottery are approximately 1 in 292 million.

→ In 1986, a man named Julio Iniguez won a state lottery and discovered he was the long-lost son of the state's governor.

→ The number 13 was considered an unlucky coincidence in the Apollo 13 mission. The mission faced a life-threatening crisis when an oxygen tank exploded. Notably, the mission launched on April 11, 1970, and encountered issues on April 13, a date often considered unlucky. The crew famously survived against the odds, turning the mission into a "successful failure."

→ Many famous musicians and artists have died at the age of 27, creating a mysterious pattern. This club includes legends like Jimi Hendrix, Janis Joplin, Jim Morrison, Kurt Cobain, and Amy Winehouse.

→ On March 12, 1961, the Dennis the Menace character debuted in the U.K. comic, The Beano. Just a few hours later a new, entirely different comic strip starring a character with the same name was published in the United States!

→ The "double birthday" phenomenon describes incidents where multiple people share the same birthday within families or groups.

→ Twins Jim Lewis and Jim Springer were separated at birth and did not meet until they were aged 39. In the meantime, both had been named James by their adoptive families, married a woman named Linda, got divorced then married again, with both their second wives named Betty. Their sons were named James Allan and James Alan, respectively!

Surprising Facts

Did you know that November 9 is the "day of fate" in Germany? It's true. Several famous or infamous events have happened on that day throughout German history. It is the date of Kaiser Wilhelm II's abdication from the throne in 1918, the end of the German monarchy, the horrors of Kristallnacht in 1938, and the fall of the Berlin Wall in 1989.

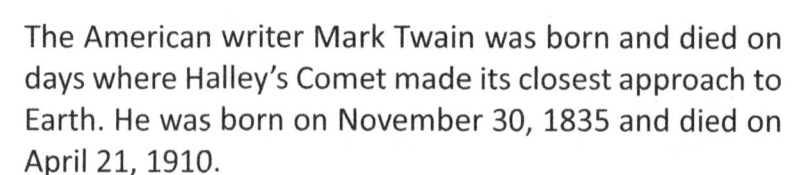

The American writer Mark Twain was born and died on days where Halley's Comet made its closest approach to Earth. He was born on November 30, 1835 and died on April 21, 1910.

Wacky World Records

Wacky world records often highlight the bizarre and unusual feats that people can achieve. These can range from the largest collection of rubber ducks to the longest time spent hula hooping or even the most spoons balanced on a person's body. Some records exist simply for their quirky nature, such as the most tattoos of a single cartoon character or the fastest time to eat a pizza while juggling. These records not only entertain but also showcase human creativity and the fun side of competition!

Here are some quirky facts about wacky world records. These records showcase the creativity and quirks found in the world of record-breaking!

→ The longest fingernails ever recorded measured over 29 feet in total length!

- The fastest time to eat a bowl of pasta is just 26.69 seconds.
- A man once balanced 18 spoons on his body at one time.
- The largest collection of garden gnomes belongs to a woman in Portugal with over 2,000 gnomes!
- The longest mustache measures over 14 feet long.
- One man jumped on a pogo stick for more than 50 hours straight.
- The most people dressed as Smurfs in one place totaled 2,762 individuals.
- The largest bubblegum bubble ever blown measured 20 inches in diameter.
- A person once walked 82 miles on stilts in 24 hours.
- The most tattoos on a single person totals over 1,000 designs.
- The longest time spent hula hooping continuously is 100 hours and 10 minutes.
- One individual holds the record for the most tattoos of the same cartoon character: Mickey Mouse.
- There exists a record for the most people dancing on ice at once, with 392 participants.
- The largest snowman ever built was 122 feet tall.
- The fastest time to assemble a Rubik's Cube is just 0.47 seconds.
- The most eggs balanced on a forehead at one time is 32.
- A group once gathered to complete the world's largest game of Twister with 1,279 players.
- The longest taco ever made measured over 717.5 feet.

- The fastest time to write "The quick brown fox jumps over the lazy dog" is 18.19 seconds.
- A chicken once flew an incredible distance of 301.5 feet!

Surprising Facts

The largest collection of rubber ducks belongs to Charlotte Lee, who has over 9,000 different rubber ducks in her collection.

Don Gorske of Wisconsin is famous for having eaten the most Big Macs in a lifetime. In 2018, he ate his 30,000th Big Mac at McDonald's, establishing a new world record.

Would you rather

- try and pronounce arachibutyrophobia (the fear of peanut butter sticking to the roof of your mouth) or hippopotomonstrosesquippedaliophobia (the fear of long words)?
- find out that your best friend is actually your sibling or share their birthday?
- compete in the International Cherry Pit-Spitting Championship in Michigan or in the Naki Sumo Crying Baby Festival in Japan to try and make babies cry?

Quiz

- ☐ What unusual law exists in Singapore about chewing gum?
- ☐ What law in Georgia involves animals and driving?
- ☐ What is arachibutyrophobia the fear of?
- ☐ Which phobia is the fear of being without your mobile phone or losing signal?
- ☐ What is the name of the phobia that involves the fear of long words?
- ☐ What is the "birthday paradox" about, and how many people need to be in a group for a 50% chance of two people sharing the same birthday?
- ☐ What unusual coincidence did marathon runner Jim McElveen and actor Tom Hanks discover about each other?

Conclusion

Hey there, young explorer!

Wow, what an awesome journey we've been on together! We've discovered some super cool facts about history, science, and nature, haven't we? From the mysteries of ancient civilizations to the wonders of the natural world and mind-blowing scientific discoveries, your curiosity has led you through a world full of fantastic fun facts.

Remember when we talked about those sneaky pharaohs in Egypt who built gigantic pyramids? How incredible is it that they used massive stones weighing tons, without any modern machines to help them? And think back to our chat about those tiny ants that can carry objects way heavier than themselves. Nature truly is amazing!

By now, you've probably impressed your friends and family with your newfound knowledge. Maybe you've even inspired someone else to put down their tablet or phone and dive into a book. That's one of the coolest things about learning—sharing what you know and sparking curiosity in others. Knowledge isn't just for keeping to yourself; it's for spreading around like confetti at a celebration!

Speaking of celebrations, did you know that reading makes your brain do a happy dance? Every time you read something new, you're giving your brain a little workout. It's like going to the gym but for your mind. Plus, because you've been reading such fascinating facts, you've made your brain stronger and more resilient. So next time you face a tricky problem, remember all those amazing facts you've learned. Your big brain can handle anything!

Let's not forget all the amazing creatures we discovered together. Imagine diving deep into the ocean to meet the bioluminescent creatures that light up like underwater fireflies. Or picture standing quietly in the rainforest, where colorful birds and exotic animals go about their day, completely unaware of how special they are. The animal kingdom is a treasure chest full of surprises just waiting for curious minds like yours to uncover them.

Science was another huge part of our adventure. From the tiniest particles to the grandest galaxies, science shows us just how vast and intricate our universe is. Did you find yourself wondering about the stars in our galaxy or how plants grow from tiny seeds into enormous trees? Every scientific fact we've explored has opened a door to even more questions, and that's the best part of science: There's always something new to discover.

So there you have it—over 1,000 facts (don't worry, we've counted)!

If ***Fabulous Fun Facts for Inquisitive Kids*** brought
some "wow" moments and big smiles to your family,
I'd love to hear your thoughts! Please consider leaving
a review to share your experience with other curious minds.

Your feedback helps spread the joy of discovery, encouraging
more young readers to dive into fun, screen-free learning
that brings the wonders of our world to life.

To leave your review, scan the QR code or simply click this link:
https://www.amazon.com/review/create-review?asin=B0DLPCC71N

Thank you for choosing this book
—warmest regards,

Violet

What Next?

But, hey, don't stop here! Just because we've reached the end of this book doesn't mean your journey has to end. It's just beginning. There are countless books out there filled with even more incredible stories and facts waiting for you. Libraries are like treasure troves, with each book holding its own set of adventures and secrets. Plus, talking to your teachers, parents, or friends about what you've learned can open up totally new conversations and ideas.

Maybe you'll be inspired to write your own book of amazing facts one day. Imagine being able to share your passion for learning with kids just like you, sparking their curiosity and helping them fall in love with reading. You've already taken the first step by exploring the wonders in this book.

Keep asking questions, keep seeking answers, and most importantly, keep having fun while you learn. The world is a vast place full of endless wonders, and with every page you turn, you're making it a little bit smaller, a little bit more familiar, and a whole lot more exciting.

So go ahead, grab your next adventure (whether it's another book, a conversation with someone interesting, or an exploration outdoors), and continue to let your inquisitive mind lead the way. You never know what fantastic fun fact you'll discover next!

Thank you for joining me on this incredible journey. Stay curious, keep reading, and let your imagination soar.

Happy adventuring, dear reader!

Quiz Answers

Want to know the answers to the quiz dotted through the book? Look no further and find the answers here!

Chapter 1

- What is the only mammal capable of sustained flight?
  Answer: The bat.

- What is the name for a group of butterflies?
  Answer: A kaleidoscope of butterflies.

- Which insect is known for its ability to fly at speeds up to 35 miles per hour?
  Answer: The dragonfly.

- What percentage of the Earth's surface is covered by the ocean?
  Answer: About 71%.

- How many hearts does an octopus have, and what color is its blood?
  Answer: Three hearts, and its blood is blue.

- What is a group of jellyfish called?
  Answer: A smack of jellyfish.

- What is the difference between amphibians and reptiles when it comes to their skin?
  Answer: Amphibians have permeable skin that absorbs water and allows them to breathe, while reptiles have dry, scaly skin that helps retain moisture.

- What special feature makes birds different from all other animals?
  Answer: Birds are the only animals with feathers.

- Which bird has the largest wingspan, and how wide is it?
  Answer: The wandering albatross has the largest wingspan, reaching up to 12 feet.

- What percentage of DNA do cats and tigers share?
  Answer: 95%.

Chapter 2

- How many times does your heart beat in a single day?
  Answer: Approximately 100,000 times.

- How much blood does your heart pump every minute? (Hint: It's enough to fill a big water bottle!)
  Answer: About 1.5 gallons.

- Even though the brain is small, how much of your body's energy does it use?
  Answer: About 20%.

- What part of the brain helps you come up with creative ideas and think outside the box?
  Answer: The right hemisphere.

- What part of your eye gets bigger or smaller depending on how much light there is?
  Answer: The pupil.

- How many different colors can your eyes see? (Hint: It's millions!)
  Answer: About 10 million.

- How many muscles does the human body have?
  Answer: Over 600 muscles.

- What part of your ear helps you keep your balance, like when you're standing on one foot?
  Answer: The vestibular system in your inner ear.

- Why does food taste so plain when your nose is stuffy?
  Answer: Because up to 80% of taste comes from your sense of smell.

- What does your stomach make to break down food and get rid of bad bacteria?
  Answer: Gastric acid (hydrochloric acid).

Chapter 3

- Is it true that plants can sleep at night?
  Answer: It is true! Plants do "sleep" at night by closing their leaves. This phenomenon is called nyctinasty.

- What is the phenomenon called when plants "sleep" by closing their leaves at night?
  Answer: Nyctinasty.

- What is the largest hot desert in the world?
  Answer: The Sahara Desert.

- Which ocean is the largest and deepest?
  Answer: The Pacific Ocean.

- Which continent holds about 70% of the world's freshwater?
  Answer: Antarctica.

- How many lightning strikes occur around the world every minute?
  Answer: Approximately 40,000.

- How much of the oxygen we breathe is produced by marine plants?
  Answer: Between 70 and 80%.

- What remarkable ability do octopuses and squids have that helps them blend into their surroundings?
  Answer: They can change the color and texture of their skin.

- What causes earthquakes, and where are they most likely to occur?
  Answer: Earthquakes are caused by the movement of tectonic plates and are most frequent at plate boundaries.

- What is the difference between a hurricane, a typhoon, and a cyclone?
  Answer: They are the same weather phenomenon but are given different names depending on where they form. Hurricanes form in the Caribbean Sea and Atlantic Ocean, typhoons in the Northwest Pacific, and cyclones in the Indian Ocean and South Pacific.

Chapter 4

- Which planet is known for having the most powerful magnetic field in the solar system?
  Answer: Jupiter.

- What is the hottest planet in the solar system?
  Answer: Venus.

- How long does it take for light from the Sun to reach Earth?
  Answer: About 8 minutes and 20 seconds.

- After our Sun, what is the closest star to Earth, and how far away is it?
  Answer: Proxima Centauri, about 4.24 light-years away.

- What happens to a massive star when it collapses under its own gravity?
  Answer: It can form a black hole.

- Which galaxy is the nearest spiral galaxy to the Milky Way?
  Answer: The Andromeda galaxy.

- What was the name of the first artificial satellite launched by the Soviet Union in 1957?
  Answer: Sputnik 1.

- Which mission successfully landed the first humans on the Moon in 1969?
  Answer: Apollo 11.

- Which planet's moon, Europa, is believed to have a subsurface ocean that could harbor life?
  Answer: Jupiter.

- What technology originally developed for military navigation is now essential for smartphones and vehicles?
  Answer: GPS technology.

Chapter 5

- Why do we get taller when we lie down at night?
  Answer: Because gravity no longer pulls us down, and our bodies are no longer compressed.

- Who discovered gravity, and what made him think about it?
  Answer: Sir Isaac Newton, after seeing an apple fall from a tree, wondered what force pulled it to the ground.

- What is the strength of an electric field measured in?
  Answer: Volts per meter (V/m).

- How does the Earth's magnetic field help protect the planet?
  Answer: It protects the planet from harmful solar radiation.

- What colors make up white light, as seen in a rainbow?
  Answer: Red, orange, yellow, green, blue, indigo, and violet.

- What type of light has a higher frequency than visible light and can cause sunburn?
  Answer: Ultraviolet light.

- How fast does sound travel compared to light in a vacuum?
  Answer: Sound travels much slower than light.

- What causes the sound of thunder?
  Answer: The rapid expansion of air heated by lightning.

- How hot can a lightning strike get?
  Answer: Around 30,000 °F.

- Why is it dangerous to be near water during a thunderstorm?
  Answer: Water is a good conductor of electricity.

Chapter 6

- What invention did Momofuku Ando create in 1958 that changed meal options globally?
  Answer: Momofuku Ando invented instant noodles in 1958, which transformed quick meal options around the world.

- Who discovered penicillin, the first antibiotic, and when did this happen?
  Answer: Alexander Fleming discovered penicillin in 1928.

- What was the purpose of the first vaccine developed by Edward Jenner in 1796?
  Answer: It was developed to combat smallpox.

- What medical invention allows doctors to perform surgery using small incisions and a camera?
  Answer: Laparoscopic surgery.

- Who invented the movable type printing press in 1454, which helped spread literature and ideas?
  Answer: Johannes Gutenberg.

- What invention by the Wright brothers in 1903 changed the way people travel across the globe?
  Answer: The airplane.

- What was the name of the first computer developed in the 1940s that weighed over 27 tons?
  Answer: ENIAC.

- Who invented the phonograph in 1877, the first device to record and playback sound?
  Answer: Thomas Edison.

- What invention did Tim Berners-Lee create in 1989 that changed how information is shared around the world?
  Answer: The World Wide Web.

- What snack was accidentally created when a chef fried very thinly sliced potatoes?
  Answer: Potato chips.

Chapter 7

- What is the name of the world's oldest known cipher and who was it named after?
  Answer: The world's oldest known cipher is the Caesar cipher. It was named after Julius Caesar.

- What number is the golden ratio (ϕ) approximately equal to?
  Answer: The golden ratio is approximately equal to 1.61803. If you got anywhere close, you can have it!

- What number is special because it has the same number of letters as the number itself?
  Answer: Four.

- In which type of sequence is each number the sum of the two previous numbers, starting with 0 and 1?
  Answer: Fibonacci sequence.

- What do we call a number that reads the same forward and backward, like 121?
  Answer: Palindrome.

- Who played a key role in breaking the Enigma code during World War II?
  Answer: Alan Turing.

- What does SOS stand for, and where is it commonly used?
  Answer: SOS doesn't stand for anything specific but is the international distress signal, especially used by ships at sea.

- **Mathematical Riddle**

  I am a three-digit number. My tens digit is five more than my ones digit. My hundreds digit is eight less than my tens digit. What number am I?

  Answer: 194

Chapter 8

- How many pounds of chocolate does the average Swiss citizen eat each year?
  Answer: In Switzerland, each person consumes an average of 24 pounds of chocolate each year. That's a lot of chocolate!

- How many hot dogs did Joey Chestnut eat in 10 minutes in 2021.
  Answer: Joey Chestnut ate 76 hot dogs in 10 minutes. Hope he didn't get indigestion afterward!

- Why do apples float in water?
  Answer: Because they are made of 25% air.

- Which vegetable used to be purple before the orange version became popular?
  Answer: Carrots.

- What fruit is called the «king of fruits» in Southeast Asia and is banned on public transport because of its strong smell?
  Answer: Durian.

- What traditional Sardinian cheese contains live insect larvae to help with fermentation?
  Answer: Casu marzu.

- Which Chinese delicacy is made from eggs preserved in a mix of clay, ash, and quicklime?
  Answer: Century eggs.

- What organization often documents official food records, like eating challenges?
  Answer: Guinness World Records.

- What unexpected spice can enhance the sweetness of ripe fruit?
  Answer: Cayenne pepper.

Chapter 9

- Which ancient civilization used brick toilet seats around 2500 B.C.E.?
  Answer: The Indus Valley Civilization.

- Who invented chocolate?
  Answer: The Mayans.

- What is the name of the legendary underwater city full of riches and amazing technology that people are still searching for?
  Answer: Atlantis.

- What is the name of the fabled gold mine in Arizona that has never been found?
  Answer: The Lost Dutchman's Gold Mine.

- Which ancient structure is the only one of the Seven Wonders of the Ancient World that remains largely intact?
  Answer: The Great Pyramid of Giza.

- Which famous aviator disappeared during a flight around the world in 1937?
  Answer: Amelia Earhart.

- What is the oldest known writing system, and who developed it?
  Answer: Cuneiform, developed by the Sumerians.

- Which writing system was used by the ancient Egyptians for over 3,000 years?
  Answer: Egyptian hieroglyphs.

- Which famous mathematician played the violin to help solve complex problems?
  Answer: Albert Einstein.

- What color was Vincent van Gogh obsessed with and often used in his paintings?
  Answer: Yellow.

Chapter 10

- What unusual law exists in Singapore about chewing gum?
  Answer: It's illegal to chew gum, except for medicinal purposes.

- What law in Georgia involves animals and driving?
  Answer: It's illegal to drive with a chicken in your lap.

- What is arachibutyrophobia the fear of?
  Answer: The fear of peanut butter sticking to the roof of your mouth.

- Which phobia is the fear of being without your mobile phone or losing signal?
  Answer: Nomophobia.

- What is the name of the phobia that involves the fear of long words?
  Answer: Hippopotomonstrosesquippedaliophobia. Anything close will do!

- What is the «birthday paradox» about, and how many people need to be in a group for a 50% chance of two people sharing the same birthday?
  Answer: It states that in a group of 23 people, there's a 50% chance that two people share the same birthday.

- What unusual coincidence did marathon runner Jim McElveen and actor Tom Hanks discover about each other?
  Answer: They had the same birthday and were born in the same hospital.

References

Allen, J. (2024). *Funky feasts: 11 weird and wonderful food festivals you've never heard of*. The Seattle Times. https://www.seattletimes.com/life/food-drink/funky-feasts-11-weird-and-wonderful-food-festivals-youve-never-heard-of/

Barrett B. (2022). Health and sustainability co-benefits of eating behaviors: Towards a science of dietary eco-wellness. *Preventive medicine reports, 28*, 101878. https://doi.org/10.1016/j.pmedr.2022.101878

Bizarre & beautiful local festivals around the world. (2024). Explore. https://www.exploreworldwide.com/blog/popular-local-festivals-around-the-world

Buchanan, R. Angus (2024, September 10). *History of technology*. Encyclopedia Britannica. https://www.britannica.com/technology/history-of-technology

Cleveland Clinic. (2022, April 29). *Blood flow through the heart*. https://my.clevelandclinic.org/health/articles/17060-how-does-the-blood-flow-through-your-heart

Cleveland Clinic. (2024, January 26). *Heart: Anatomy & function*. https://my.clevelandclinic.org/health/body/21704-heart

Cole, G. G., Millett, A. C., & Juanchich, M. (2024). The social learning account of trypophobia. *Quarterly Journal of Experimental Psychology, 0*(0). https://doi.org/10.1177/17470218241232665

Debnath, L. A brief history of the most remarkable numbers π, g and δ in mathematical sciences with applications. *Int. J. Appl. Comput. Math 1*, 607–638 (2015). https://doi.org/10.1007/s40819-015-0038-6

ENTO 2010E ultimate quizlet flashcards. (n.d.). Quizlet. https://quizlet.com/658728643/ento-2010e-ultimate-quizlet-flash-cards/

Erkan. (2024, July 8). *10 most intriguing lost civilizations and their legacies*. The Most 10 of Everything. https://www.themost10.com/intriguing-lost-civilizations-and-their-legacies/

FasterCapital. (n.d.). *Symmetry: FibonacciFan: The symmetrical magic in numbers update.* https://fastercapital.com/content/Symmetry--FibonacciFan--The-Symmetrical-Magic-in-Numbers-update.html

Garber, M. (2012, September 14). *The 20 most significant inventions in the history of food and drink.* The Atlantic. https://www.theatlantic.com/technology/archive/2012/09/the-20-most-significant-inventions-in-the-history-of-food-and-drink/262410/

Goodley, A. (2024, August 25). *14 mythical lost treasures yet to be discovered.* Rarest.org. https://rarest.org/entertainment/mythical-lost-treasures-yet-to-be-discovered

Hayes, J. (2017, May 12). *The Victorian belief that a train ride could cause instant insanity.* Atlas Obscura. https://www.atlasobscura.com/articles/railway-madness-victorian-trains

Hogg, P. (2021, June 21). *The top 10 medical advances in history.* Proclinical. https://www.proclinical.com/blogs/2021-6/the-top-10-medical-advances-in-history

How intelligent are whales and dolphins? (2019). Whale and Dolphin Conservation. https://us.whales.org/whales-dolphins/how-intelligent-are-whales-and-dolphins/

Huang, Y., & Wen, Z. (2016). *The structure of palindromes in the Fibonacci sequence and some applications.* ResearchGate. https://www.researchgate.net/publication/291229527_The_structure_of_palindromes_in_the_Fibonacci_sequence_and_some_applications

Janik V. M. (2014). Cetacean vocal learning and communication. *Current opinion in neurobiology, 28,* 60–65. https://doi.org/10.1016/j.conb.2014.06.010

Lawlor D. W. (2009). Musings about the effects of environment on photosynthesis. *Annals of botany, 103*(4), 543–549. https://doi.org/10.1093/aob/mcn256

Lazarus, R. (2020, October 11). *How does the eye work?* Optometrists Network. https://www.optometrists.org/general-practice-optometry/guide-to-eye-health/how-does-the-eye-work/

Lemon, J. (2023, June 21). *The astonishing diversity of life: Exploring the wonders of the ocean.* Ocean Partners. https://www.ocean-partners.org/portfolio/the-astonishing-diversity-of-life-exploring-the-wonders-of-the-ocean/

Levin, A. (2020, March 26). *Trending ingredients and techniques for a new era of baked goods.* Prepared Foods. https://www.preparedfoods.com/articles/123651-trending-ingredients-and-techniques-for-a-new-era-of-baked-goods

Lorenz, L. (2024). *Evolution of insects cartoons and comics.* CartoonStock. https://www.cartoonstock.com/directory/e/evolution_of_insects.asp

Marilyn vos Savant. (2014). Geniuses. https://geniuses.club/genius/marilyn-vos-savant

Mastinu, M., Mells, M., Yousaf, N. Y., Barbarossa, I. T., & Tepper, B. J. (2023). Emotional responses to taste and smell stimuli: Self-reports, physiological measures, and a potential role for individual and genetic factors. *Journal of Food Science, 88* (51). https://ift.onlinelibrary.wiley.com/doi/full/10.1111/1750-3841.16300

NASA. (2023a, September 22). *Why go to space.* https://www.nasa.gov/humans-in-space/why-go-to-space/

NASA. (2023b, September 28). *Galaxies over time.* https://science.nasa.gov/mission/webb/galaxies-over-time/

NASA. (2024, August 1). *Stars.* https://science.nasa.gov/universe/stars/

National Eye Institute. (2022, April 20). *How the eyes work.* https://www.nei.nih.gov/learn-about-eye-health/healthy-vision/how-eyes-work

National Geographic. (n.d.-a). *All about climate.* https://education.nationalgeographic.org/resource/all-about-climate/

National Geographic. (n.d.-b). *Weather.* https://www.nationalgeographic.org/encyclopedia/weather

National Park Service. (2022, November 16). *Plant adaptations.* https://www.nps.gov/teachers/classrooms/plant-adaptations.htm

NRICH. (n.d.) *Recommended books.* https://nrich.maths.org/recommended-books

Osmosis. (2024, March 28). *The top 10 medical advances in history*. https://www.osmosis.org/blog/2023/07/10/the-top-10-medical-advances-in-history

Paine, R. D. (2021, March 12). *The book of buried treasure: True story of the pirate gold and jewels*. Everand. https://www.everand.com/book/498490413/The-Book-of-Buried-Treasure-True-Story-of-the-Pirate-Gold-and-Jewels

Parkhurst Ferguson, P. (2014). Inside the extreme sport of competitive eating. *Contexts, 13*(3), 26-31. https://doi.org/10.1177/1536504214545756

Pedersen, T. (2021, December 21). *Trypophobia: Symptoms, causes, triggers, and more*. Psych Central. https://psychcentral.com/anxiety/trypophobia

Pi gets all the fanfare, but other numbers also deserve their own math holidays. (2023, March 8). UMBC. https://umbc.edu/stories/pi-gets-all-the-fanfare-but-other-numbers-also-deserve-their-own-math-holidays/

Poirot, L., & Sulc, B. A. (2024, May 22). *60 weird laws around the world*. Far and Wide. https://www.farandwide.com/s/weird-laws-world-4961c1ede8d749bf

Ramos, A. (2023, June). *The world-famous list of weird foods that people eat*. Andreas.com. https://andreas.com/weird-food.html

Rank, M. (2013). *Lost civilizations: 10 societies that vanished without a trace*. CreateSpace

Saraiva, A., Carrascosa, C., Raheem, D., Ramos, F., & Raposo, A. (2020). Natural sweeteners: The relevance of food naturalness for consumers, food security aspects, sustainability and health impacts. *International journal of environmental research and public health, 17*(17), 6285. https://doi.org/10.3390/ijerph17176285

Scott, K. (2024, March 6). *Animals of the ocean depths*. Oceana. https://oceana.org/blog/animals-of-the-ocean-depths/

7 innovations that changed food safety. (2021, March 24). Manufacturing Business Technology. https://www.mbtmag.com/industry-4-0/article/21342727/7-innovations-that-changed-food-safety

Signe, L., & Dooley, H. (2023, March 28). *How space exploration is fueling the Fourth Industrial Revolution*. Brookings. https://www.brookings.edu/articles/how-space-exploration-is-fueling-the-fourth-industrial-revolution/

10 weird laws from around the world. (2023, March 13). The Lawyer Portal. https://www.thelawyerportal.com/blog/top-10-weirdest-laws-around-world/

The world's oldest ancient feats of engineering will amaze you. (2024, February 27). Loveexploring.com. https://www.loveexploring.com/gallerylist/142140/the-worlds-oldest-ancient-feats-of-engineering-will-amaze-you

Unique and unusual food and drink. (2024). Atlas Obscura. https://www.atlasobscura.com/unique-food

University of Illinois. (n.d.-a). *Gravity vs. magnetism*. https://van.physics.illinois.edu/ask/listing/225

University of Illinois. (n.d.-b). *Light and magnets... and gravity*. https://van.physics.illinois.edu/ask/listing/2009

Vorvick, L. J. (2023, February 2). *Body temperature norms*. MedlinePlus. https://medlineplus.gov/ency/article/001982.htm

White, A. (2024, July 10). *Incredible feats of ancient engineering that will blow your mind*. MSN. https://www.msn.com/en-ca/travel/tripideas/incredible-feats-of-ancient-engineering-that-will-blow-your-mind/ss-BB1pHorS

Made in United States
North Haven, CT
23 April 2025